Living a Blissful Marriage

24 Steps to Happiness

Lilian Gafni

First Edition

Lifeline Publishing
Rancho Palos Verdes, California

Living a Blissful Marriage
24 Steps to Happiness

Published by:
Lifeline Publishing
Post Office Box 4689
Palos Verdes Peninsula, California 90274

Copyright © 2001 by Lilian Gafni
ISBN: 0-9702735-0-9
Library of Congress Control Number: 00-93200

First Printing 2001

Printed in the United States of America
10 9 8 7 6 5 4 3 2 1

To my husband Joel for his love
and
To our children David and Ilana for allowing me to give all my
attention to this book

Note to the Reader

The purpose of this book is to give insights to couples who feel they still love each other and want to preserve their marriage despite their marital problems, and are willing to try every possible option to make their marriage work. This book is intended to educate those couples in acquiring knowledge and practical solutions for the problems in their marriage, with the ultimate goal of achieving bliss in their marriage by working daily to nurture it.

This book is not intended for treating individuals or couples with severe emotional problems such as addictions or physical and sexual abuse. Those problems should be referred to a qualified therapist in the field.

Every effort has been made to make this manual as complete and as accurate as possible. However, there may be mistakes both typographical and in content. Therefore, this text should be used only as a general guide and not as the ultimate source on marriage advice.

Lifeline Publishing and the author shall have no responsibility nor liability to any person regarding loss or damage caused, or alleged to be caused, directly or undirectly by the information in this book.

Acknowledgments

To acknowledge all the authorities, sources and individuals who have contributed to the making of this book would require an entire text. However, I would like to acknowledge specific individuals and groups but for whom this book might not have become a reality.

My gratitude goes to my copy editor, Virginia Iorio, for the many hours she spent on the manuscript to improve it and to give it a satisfying final shape. A special thanks goes to Donna Lee Braunstein and her detective skills, in obtaining permissions from the many publishing houses for the quotes appearing in the book.

Many thanks go to Louise Barr, Wes Greayer, Dave Kenney, Jack King, Bill Lashbrook, Tom Mooney, Martha Morehead, John Nursall, Jean Shriver, Cat Spydell, and Dave Turner of the Palos Verdes Writer's Workshop who spent many Tuesdays listening and making suggestions on the manuscript. A special thank you is due to Marjeanne Blinn, Sylvia Richardson, Lanny Swallow and Phil Wesley from the staff at the Palos Verdes Library for their unrelenting help to locate facts and data. I want to express my sincerest gratitude to Irene Berlin, Rabbi Eli Hecht, Professor David Levy, and Amy Montague for their valuable psychological and spiritual advice.

I sincerely want to thank the many publishing houses for their graceful permission to reprint copyrighted material and poetry quotes from their books. A list of publishers and their publications is found in the reference pages at the end of this book.

Cover Photo by Barbara A. Wood
   Courtship: Oil on canvas

Copyediting by Virginia Iorio

Cover and page design by One-On-One Book
   Production, West Hills, CA

Permissions

Excerpts from *Beneath the Mask: An Introduction to Theories of Personality*, Fourth Edition. Copyright © 1991 by Christopher Monte. Reprinted by permission of Harcourt, Inc.

Excerpts from "Dream Deferred" and "Still Here" from *Collected Poems* by Langston Hughes. Copyright © 1994 by the Estate of Langston Hughes. Reprinted by permission of Alfred A. Knopf, a Division of Random House Inc.

Excerpts from *The Ego and the Id* by Sigmund Freud, translated by Joan Riviere. Translation copyright © 1960 by James Strachey, renewed 1988 by Alix Strachey. Reprinted by permission of W. W. Norton & Company.

Excerpts from *The Ego and Mechanisms of Defense* by Anna Freud. Copyright © 1966 by International Universities Press, Inc.

Excerpts from *Foundations of Physiological Psychology*, Third Edition by Neil R. Carlson. Copyright © 1995 by Allyn & Bacon. Reprinted/adapted by permission of Allyn & Bacon.

Excerpts from *Inhibitions, Symptoms and Anxiety* by Sigmund Freud, translated by Alix Strachey. Translation copyright © 1959 by Alex Strachey. Reprinted by permission of W. W. Norton & Company.

Excerpts from *Merriam-Webster's Collegiate® Dictionary, Tenth Edition*. Copyright © 2000 by Merriam-Webster, Incorporated. Reprinted by permission of Merriam-Webster, Incorporated.

Excerpts from *Mistress of the House, Mistress of Heaven: Women in Ancient Egypt* by Anne K. Capel and Glenn E. Markoe, Editors. Essays by Catharine H. Roehrig, Betsy M. Bryan, and Janet H. Johnson. Copyright © 1996 by Cincinnati Art Museum. Used by permission of the publisher, Hudson Hills Press.

Excerpts from *Our Sexuality*, Fifth Edition by Robert Crooks and Karla Baur. Copyright © 1993 by Brooks/Cole Publishing Company. An International Thompson Publishing Company.

Excerpts from *The Small Woman* by Alan Burgess. Copyright © 1957 by E. P. Dutton, renewed © 1985 by Alan Burgess. Used by permission of Dutton, a division of Penguin Putnam Inc.

Excerpt from *The Star Trek Compendium* by Allan Asherman. Copyright © 1989 by Paramount Pictures Corporation and Copyright © by Pocket Books, a division of Simon and Schuster, Inc.

Excerpts from *The Stepford Wives* by Ira Levin. Copyright © 1972 by Ira Levin. Used by permission of Random House, Inc. and Random House of Canada Limited.

Table of Contents

PART I: THE COCOON

PART II: THE CATERPILLAR

PART III: THE BUTTERFLY

List of Exercises

List of Tables

About the Author

Lilian Gafni, through her life experiences, became acutely aware of the unhappiness, breakups and heartaches of many failed marriages. Realizing that what was generally offered in literature on marriage advice was limited, she formulated a unique on-going approach — that an everyday reminder, a special kind of conditioning and exercises could make the major difference in many marriages.

Through her research, observations, experiences, and psychology background Lilian introduces couples to key steps they can take on an everyday basis to maintain a wonderful relationship and a blissful marriage.

Lilian Gafni's life has been varied and exciting. She began her education in Cairo, Egypt, served in the Israeli armed forces and eventually came to the United States where she expanded her education at Portland State University in Oregon and then Pepperdine University, California with studies in Clinical Psychology.

She has written a book of poetry, *Swing into the Sky*, and two novels, *The Trans-Siberian Express* and the award winning (International Literary Awards), *Hello Exile*.

She and her husband of forty years have two children and currently reside in Southern California.

Preface

There was a child went forth every day, And the first object he looked upon and received with wonder or pity or love or dread, that object he became, And that object became part of him for the day or a certain part of the day ... or for many years or stretching cycles of years.

—Walt Whitman

Marriage can be described as a work of art in progress. And as a work in progress, its fulfillment depends closely upon the partners' creative interaction with each other, their shared contributions to that union, and most importantly, each one's unique personality.

Each partner's personality can then be compared to a precious diamond trapped in solid rock and yearning to release the sparkle buried inside. There is such a diamond in all of us waiting to reflect our essence — our hunger for love, our need to be understood and our thirst to spread the love locked inside us.

Yes, a woman longs for her man to respond in kind to her tenderness, and a man yearns to unleash in his woman a love and passion for him. We all search for that special someone. That search motivates us to embark on a voyage of discovery and fuse with another to find bliss.

Bliss in marriage represents a peaceful and harmonious state of life where conflicts can become resolved by applying the knowledge and tools you will find in this book. The peaceful environment existing in a blissful marriage is one where both spouses feel safe in their trust toward each other, and in the security that their needs will be listened to without undue criticism.

Once the partners have transcended the disharmony of a conflictful marriage with its share of anxieties, alienation and anger, a blissful marriage allows them to focus and build a foundation of mutual support, and to merge with one another to create a future where only growth occurs.

This growth depends on the partners' personalities, which can be as complex as the many facets of a diamond. They can include childhood imprinting, behavior resulting from early role-modeling, family influences, individual thought patterns, attitudes toward money, and social role expectations. Those factors can contribute to the marriage by bringing either disharmony or a life-building legacy to the union.

Accordingly, the history of psychology has taught us that human behavior is influenced by a complexity of early impressions in life, and by observing the role-modeling of significant adults in our lives. In early childhood we learned about the immediate world around us by observing and recording the established rules in our brain. If a negative behavior was encoded by our sight, hearing or sense of smell, then this behavior became the "blueprint" for our later actions or thoughts. As infants and children, we were unable to comprehend guidelines or evaluate which behaviors were socially appropriate and beneficial for our welfare. Without knowing the acceptable social rules of conduct, we could not correct those first impressions. They became permanent blueprints in our brain and we have no eraser to wipe them out. We can only correct those first impressions by placing them now in their proper perspective.

As we grew up and acquired a wealth of information about life, we then had the tools for making life decisions. If we lacked the proper role model, we were left to hit-and-miss interpretations of life. However, now as responsible adults, we have the free will and the option to change our behavior if it is detrimental to our welfare and our full enjoyment of life.

It is the purpose of this book to help you examine and change the many factors that may keep you from achieving a blissful marriage.

Now take a pen and a journal, and jot down thoughts, memories and feelings that are triggered as you read this book. Keep a running journal with each chapter until you have read the last page. You will be asked to write in your journal as part of the twenty-four exercises that help you to apply what you learn in each chapter.

If you read the entire book and do the exercises only afterward, you will be doing yourself a disservice. You should do the exercises as you encounter them in each chapter, and then set aside five minutes each day to review them. To get the full benefit of this book, these exercises must be done daily, and gradually mastered by repetition. Your first exercise will begin with Chapter 1. For example, you will read Chapter 1, read the exercise, close the book, and practice the exercise, in that sequence. Do not read Chapter 2 until you have practiced the exercise in Chapter 1. Follow the same procedure for each exercise whether it is in the middle or at the end of a chapter. If any chapter has two consecutive exercises, practice them before you go on to the next chapter.

Buy some three-by-five-inch, lined index cards, and keep them accessible for summarizing your thoughts, as directed in the exercises. Keep the notes short and focused so you don't become sidetracked or indulge in past hurts.

In the genealogical chart found at the end of the book, you will write your family characteristics in the blanks when the designated exercise tells you to do so.

I strongly urge both you and your spouse to participate in reading this book and doing the exercises. The marriage bond is enhanced when both partners understand reactions to behaviors, as well as how and what to communicate when interacting with each other. Become active partners as you read this book and empower yourselves to change your destiny.

At one time or another everyone has stumbling blocks in their relationship, but as you learn throughout this book to decipher complex human behaviors, you can prevent these pitfalls in your marriage. This book is also for the partners who have lost the purpose and special spark that once united two people who were very much in love. Silence and alienation usually take place in the denial that problems exist. A bitter resignation then sets in where oceanic bliss once existed, and two people fall out of love. This book can help you only if you want to change old habits to rediscover the magnetic attraction that drew you close together.

This book will not teach you everything there is to know about the relationship with your spouse, because you are the only teacher in this marriage and in how you want your relationship to evolve. This is only a workbook to guide and give you the working tools you need to make your marriage grow. As your relationship goes through the struggles and conflicts of married life, small changes will occur that will change you, and change the relationship accordingly. Additionally, this book will help you rediscover your own psyche—the person you really are and your soul's wishes—and find the commonality and humanity you share with your spouse. With each chapter you will keep in mind alternatives and visions of a better life together. As changes occur, slowly at first then at a faster rate, you will see your relationship with greater understanding and compassion, and that will restore the love and sense of purpose to your marriage.

Briefly, this is what marriage is all about: the ability to adapt with changing times in a couple's life. A formidable task is then laid before us when we make this lifetime voyage in commitment. Together you and your spouse will explore these uncharted waters and through the unknown find your way to love in a safe harbor.

You and I

We meet as strangers, each carrying a mystery
within us. I cannot say who you are.
But I trust that you are a person in your own
right, possessed of a beauty and value that are
the Earth's richest treasures.
So I make this promise to you:

I will impose no identities upon you, but will
invite you to become yourself
without shame or fear.

I will hold open a space for you in the world and
allow your right to fill it with an authentic vocation
and purpose.

For as long as your search
takes, you have my loyalty.

— Unknown

Introduction

The Road to
Understanding Marriage

Two roads diverged in a wood, and I—
I took the one less traveled by,
And that has made all the difference.

—Robert Frost

What does the road to understanding marriage mean? Does it come automatically with the marriage license, or does it happen gradually within the marriage? After many years of living with one's spouse, partners know each other's thoughts and develop patterns of mutual understanding. These couples also experience conflicts and disagreements in their relationship but learn how to face those hurdles. Other couples do not know how to resolve their problems and choose instead the road to separation.

What then does it take to avoid pitfalls, and where is the shortcut to a healthy marriage? The answer lies in our conception of marriage and what it means to us. For many of us, marriage symbolizes the end of an unhappy childhood or the end of a lifelong search for the perfect partner. This partner will make it all right for us and undo all the wrongs. In our ideal conception of a mate, we design in our mind the type of person our spouse will be: the man of my dreams, tall, handsome, passionate and fabulously rich; or the woman of my dreams with the perfect face and body, the understanding and patience of a nun, and the sexual prowess of a goddess. Nowhere in our design for that mate do we ask ourselves what we can do or bring to make our mate happy.

Many times our conception of love and mutual understanding comes from what we have learned in early life and seen all around us. These guidelines from our early years can be powerful in influencing the entire course of a lifetime. As infants we observed our parents' behavior, the verbal or concealed message of expectations they had for us, as well as the behavior of others around us. These behaviors, messages or cues were integrated into our personality to become part of us forever.

We can visualize the mind of an infant as a blank slate but having a wealth of brain cells, called neurons, similar to the back panel of a highly sophisticated computer. These neurons, however, are still unconnected by their synapses, or the communication connections between neurons. Along with this "hardware," the infant comes equipped with a multitude of burgeoning emotions that integrate feelings and perceptions as they are gradually experienced. We can compare the infant to a human who has accidentally landed on an alien planet. This human will first observe all the moves and behavior of the alien population, and study any cues foreshadowing danger.

Since survival is the goal for the human infant, he or she will adapt to the surrounding environment. When hunger begins to stir, the infant will listen to the sounds around the crib and begin a call for attention with plaintive sighs. The infant will then cry louder if the call for attention goes unnoticed. In that manner the infant will keep on trying until a time comes when resignation sets in, or he or she falls asleep from exhaustion. Through all the years of life, the infant within the young child or adult will also call for attention or help when unable to cope with the environment. This call for help can take the form of unusual behavior when those around him or her are not listening. When no response is forthcoming, either destructive behavior or resignation in the form of depression sets in. In some marriages, this resignation can lead to spiritual death.

How can we find or rediscover the love and ideal companion we have searched for all our lives? We begin by first discarding our old expectations and then building a new idea of marriage. We have to examine whether our expectations are realistic and ask ourselves why we want that particular mate. We can then eliminate the unrealistic image of an ideal mate and substitute in its place an individual with desires, hopes and aspirations that are common to us all. It is when we can see these human qualities in our partner that we find love. This love is a mirror image of what we have projected onto our spouse. It is when we feel compassion and respect for our spouse as a person with feelings and rights of their own that this love grows and comes back to us. The love we seek in our mate results from the love we give to them. Without first giving that love, it would be like expecting water to flow from a rock or flowers to spring forth from desert sand.

This book therefore examines the questions, the myths, the fears, the misconceptions, the illusions, the anticipation and the expectations of marriage. We can then breathe life and love into a mate who has died spiritually.

Part I
THE COCOON

— 1 —

The Beginning

Know Thyself

—Socrates

You are now ready for a voyage of discovery into marriage. Marriage can be a combination of all sorts of things. It can begin with the need to continue a romantic adventure and mutual attraction through common interests. It could also begin as a sexual attraction: the mystery of discovery through another person's soul or psyche, and through the communion of two bodies yearning to fuse into one being.

More often than not, marriage is the ultimate search for that special someone who will validate who we are and make us whole again. This special someone will make us forget any lonely or wretched childhood memories of times past, and make us feel special for the first time in our life. Sometimes the companionship of two close friends can turn to romantic love that prompts them to tie the knot. This type of marriage usually begins with two people feeling safe together. The safety net they share is a gentle meeting of two minds accepting each other's thoughts and behavior. That acceptance is the mutual trust of a friend committed not only to your safety but also to your growth.

Marriage then is the union of two people who are very much in love as well as the discovery of a friend for life. This friend will stand by you, believe in you and validate your existence by making your world a safe haven. There is an all-encompassing reason why we get married. It is more than what appears on the surface, such as common background or physical attraction; it is two souls connecting in a permanent bond.

Biological reproduction is another reason for getting married and the natural progression of leaving one's mark on this earth while extending oneself indefinitely by living through one's children. To give life to another being is the ultimate gift: the chance for another to breathe and feel life. The joys of having children are immeasurable when two people are willing to postpone, temporarily, their own comfort for the sake of that new life. These sacrifices become bearable, however, when the parents have had their own needs met. That means they have achieved a certain measure of satisfaction in life, and the assurance that they are loved by their spouse through mutual affection and caring for one another. It also means they have reached a satisfactory level of professional success, and enjoy reasonable financial comfort in their day-to-day life.

The miracle of life can take on a marvelous dimension when the parents' needs are satisfied in a successful and blissful marriage. That happens when two people fall in love and, with optimum conditions, their lives follow a pattern through the years of progressive growth. Life does not work ideally, however, for most of us. We may get married very young, before having had the opportunity to establish careers and financial security. We may also bring into the marriage "suitcases" filled with a painful past. Obstacles then become stumbling blocks to a couple whose intentions were well meant at the start.

What are these stumbling blocks and where do they come from? These roadblocks in a marriage may have been strewn a long time ago. They may have begun when each spouse was but an infant in their parents' arms. In each family's history these roadblocks are disguised, appearing on the surface as natural, common events. An example of such an event that may plant the seeds for the undoing of a couple's chance for happiness would be a man's inability to find employment, and subsequent frustration in his attempts to secure a future for himself and his family. That's not to say that in every case of unemployment a dysfunction will lead to unhappiness or misery. However, it may contribute to the unraveling of a marriage by directly applying the force of a downward spiral.

Let's take the case history of Sydney and Sarah.

∾ ∾ ∾

A Case Study

The year is 1910 when they marry. Soon after, the young couple brings into the world two children: first a boy, Ben, then a year later a girl, Alise. Uneducated, Sydney decides to take employment on a ship to support his family. Sarah pleads with him to be patient, that something else is bound to turn up. Tired of waiting, Sydney enlists on a fishing freighter for one year. Sarah, who resigns herself after her in-laws advise her not to stand in the way of her husband's progress, says good-bye to Sydney while Ben and Alise clutch at her skirt.

The first monthly paychecks soon begin to arrive, helping Sarah pay the rent and put food on the table. Then the paychecks arrive every two months, and after seven months no more money comes. Sarah tries to contact the shipyard's office but the manager is out every time, and her in-laws, being poor, cannot help her.

The year is now 1915. World War I is in full swing and Sarah has not heard from Sydney for one year. Meanwhile, Sarah has taken in laundry and ironing to keep her small family alive. Ben is now four years old and takes care of his sister by feeding and watching over her while Sarah struggles with her laundry load. Ben, a reserved boy, grows up with no father and no attention from Sarah, who becomes paler and more downtrodden every day.

The war ends and life continues for the three, when one day Sydney shows up. Nothing changes for the family except that now Sydney is drinking heavily and abuses all three by terrorizing them when he comes home drunk: the table is overturned and chairs hurled at walls while Sarah tries to protect the children. In this atmosphere of fear for their safety, the children learn to hate their father, and Ben swears never to touch alcohol. Sarah then becomes gradually disabled with Parkinson's disease. Now Ben has an alcoholic and violent father who works occasionally, and a mother who's ill and emotionally unavailable.

Disabled by a leg injury and lacking education, Ben marries at the age of twenty-three. He is crazy about his beautiful wife, Reneé, and becomes jealous of anyone who looks at her. Ben, also an angry man, fathers three children, who become the brunt of his nervous and violent nature. He hits his children and calls John, his oldest son, "Hitler" because of John's habit of pinching children and hitting his younger sister and brother. John grows up, marries, then makes his new wife miserable by accusing her of flirting and confining her to the home. Years later, John's wife divorces him and gets custody of their two children.

∽ख़   ∽ख़   ∽ख़

This family history follows the pattern of a despondent father in the first generation, abandonment that breeds repressed anger and hate in the second generation, and a son who feels no worth in the third generation, leading to a divorce. If every case were that simple, we would have the one and only formula for conflict resolution in marital discord and a clear road to a blissful marriage. But no two cases are alike; every case is unique as each individual has patterns of thoughts, comprehension and interpretation of their own. In most cases, however, a pattern or theme of family problems can be found in the genealogical history.

The Lessons of the Odyssey

In Homer's *Odyssey*, Odysseus has been sailing for ten years on a voyage of self-discovery. Meanwhile back home, his wife, Penelope, is longing for his return. She occupies her time by unraveling and reweaving the same shroud over and over (an obsessive-compulsive occupation to repress the longing for her husband). In the meantime, his son, Telemachus, is forced to protect the home and grow up without a father.

What does this mythic story tell us? Is it that every man has to go through an initiation rite of passage or a voyage into self-discovery? Or that every man longing for an absent father will feel compelled to travel a lifetime and learn about life the hard way? I believe the latter is self-explanatory. In every family where a father becomes absent through life's hardships or through a yearning for his own father, the result in the ensuing generations is a pattern of trying to fill a bottomless void. To fill this void, a man will explore the world around him through adventurous or dangerous extramarital relationships, alienate himself from his family or retreat into himself.

For a woman, the father she missed having can chain her forever to an infinite search for the perfect man. This perfect male will give her all imagined satisfactions she yearned for while growing up: being cherished and admired as the only girl in a man's life, safety and companionship. Of course, all of these qualities in a man should be part of the natural father-daughter relationship when optimum conditions exist in the family home. Unfortunately, that has not been the norm in our past or present society.

Early Role-Modeling

A woman's most cherished dream in marriage is not only to live harmoniously with her mate, but also to provide for the complete well-being of their children, both physical and emotional. If a woman has grown up in a thriving atmosphere where every one of her steps was guided with care and love, she will want to duplicate those conditions when she gets married.

If instead she grew up in a tense, violent or abusive home, she will consciously want the opposite in her marriage; unconsciously, however, she will duplicate her home of origin. While she may know exactly what she does not want in a companion for life, she has no clue as to the opposite. If, during the critical years of her upbringing when the imprinting of impressions became etched into her brain, the role-modeling she perceived at home was lacking in love and affection between her father and mother, she will unconsciously allow the same conditions to be reproduced in her marriage. It is only when we have felt and lived through love that we can express it freely and unconditionally.

The role-modeling we observed as children becomes our guide into adulthood. We learned that to get love, we had to meet certain expectations: being good, giving of ourselves, sharing our possessions with others, learning to decipher our parents' moods and cues to please them. We made our own assumptions about love based on their behavior toward us, and built an image of ourselves according to the adult role models in the home. Every boy and girl naturally wants to grow up to be just like their father and mother, but if our father or mother displays negative or destructive behavior, we will hate this behavior, deny it, and try to keep it out of our conscious awareness. This behavior becomes imprinted into our unconsciousness, however, and will plague us in later years.

Take, for example, a boy who grew up in an alcoholic home where the father abused his wife or children. That boy will imprint the image of a hateful father and may very well duplicate that image in himself as an adult—or go to the opposite extreme, as in the following case history.

A Case Study

Brad had an alcoholic father who terrorized his mother and brothers. He witnessed the subjugation of his mother by his father's bullying attitude and behavior. Brad then grew up to hate and fear his father. He swore that as a grown man he would never touch alcohol as long as he lived.

In his adult years, Brad kept his promise. He married in his early twenties and fathered three children. Brad stayed away from bars, avoided social events for fear of having to face liquor, and made his wife's life lonely with no social contact. She grew to despise him and took the upper hand in rearing their children. As she became the dominant partner in the family, he retreated into passivity. Brad could not challenge his wife. It would have been like raising his voice to his own mother, just as his father had.

Brad's extreme determination not to duplicate the role-modeling of his father nonetheless had negative results in his life.

The Masks We Wear

In ancient Greece different masks represented the many emotions displayed by actors in a drama, such as rage, anger or grief. Those masks had a metallic mouthpiece through which the voice of the actor resonated. Later on, the Romans called the mask *per sonare*, meaning "to sound through." This Latin term is the root of our word persona, meaning both the role that an actor plays and the public image that we display in society (Monte, 1991).

When the custom of masked balls became fashionable in society, the mask helped to conceal one's identity until the end of the ball. The participants fantasized about their partner's identity and delighted in its mystery. In the meantime, the masked figure felt anonymity or concealment behind its facade. The purpose of the mask therefore was to conceal the true personality, as one "really is." We do much the same in our everyday life when we try to conceal our true feelings, or who we really are.

What is it exactly that we are trying hard to hide? Is it the vulnerable person inside us? Is it the person we want to protect, or the person we do not want to reveal? Why do we hide who we really are? Perhaps we hide our feelings to protect them from further injury and rejection. If you go back in time and examine your childhood and youth, ask yourself, what are the things that motivated you, and when and why did they become hidden?

Children grow up daily in a testing environment. They see, hear and model every day's events. For example, young children will learn new words every day — that is, if they are exposed to an active verbal environment. Likewise, they will observe adult behaviors and incorporate those as their own. Young children have no capacity to judge between right and wrong. They will see a behavior and copy it.

If children are hindered from expressing themselves, they will internalize this restriction and keep themselves in check every time an opportunity arises to be creative. After so many self-checks, this lid on creativity will become permanent and part of their conditioning. How many times have you seen a form of art such as painting, dancing or singing, and thought to yourself, "I am not a good dancer" or "I can't hold a tune."

At times in your childhood you might have seen a positive behavior you wanted to imitate, but were prevented from doing so because it seemed dangerous to your parent or guardian or was not deemed appropriate at the time. All those wishes and desires you had as a child or young adolescent that were stopped or discouraged will become part of your psyche, and as an adult you will not need your parent or guardian to stop you. You will unconsciously and automatically stop yourself.

All those budding wishes and desires that were repressed will remain locked inside you forever. They may resurface now and then, triggered by some event, but a sigh will escape you, and back again they will be repressed. Any significant wish that has been repressed will always be there in your memory or in your unconscious. Any wish that was not resolved or replaced by another worthwhile endeavor will fester and prevent you from achieving new endeavors. You will expend a great amount of energy to avoid thinking about the loss you experienced. You will use every bit available to protect that memory from resurfacing and to avoid feeling the pain associated with that loss. Since human energies are finite, that is where your energy quota will run short and prevent you from focusing your strength into the proper channels.

Therefore this lost youth may become a hindrance as the years go by and interfere with self-growth and relationships. A sure sign of paralysis of will is always looking back, regretting missed opportunities in the past. This paralysis prevents you from living in the moment. That is not to say that we have to close the door on the past, but rather to use these missed chances by learning from them to improve the future and become more fully the person we were meant to be.

Freud's Theory of Personality

If we can see how our thought patterns affect our interpretation of life events, and our subsequent behavior following that interpretation, we can then understand why we are complex creatures.

In 1923, Sigmund Freud constructed a theory of the mind and its functioning. In his theory the mind is governed by three subsystems: the Id, the Ego and the Superego. The Id, being the oldest part of our personality, represents the infant and child in us and the unconscious goal of immediate wish fulfillment. The Ego is the adult or conscious personality that brings order from the Id's chaos. The Superego represents our identification with and internalization of our parents' character.

All three entities sometimes clash within us and attempt to dominate our behavior. The Id, in its quest for instant gratification, can overpower the Ego. The Ego will then try to mediate a compromise, and the Superego will moralize or induce a guilty conscience. When the Id is in a constant demand phase it overpowers the Ego, which becomes weaker and powerless to bring order. The Superego, on the other hand, will be the conscience passing judgment on the Id by punishing it. In this model of three subsystems, homeostasis is the key and the answer to equilibrium in our lives. By being fully conscious of our behavior and motivations, we can see why we hold on to old destructive habits and can become better able to correct them.

In relationships and in marriage, communication break-downs are often the result of our mostly unconscious desire for immediate wish fulfillment. We want prompt attention to our needs, and we sometimes fail to recognize that our partner also has needs that prevent him or her from paying immediate attention to our needs. We then automatically think of our partner as uncaring. The tendency to see only one's own needs can be the source of much conflict. If we can instead train ourselves to acknowledge and attend to our spouse's needs first, we will eliminate these sources of future problems.

The next section of this chapter will show you a way to train your mind to satisfy both your needs and those of your spouse. It will also help you better understand your partner and establish the foundation for a loving relationship between the two of you.

Visual Imagery for Merging with Your Spouse

What does it feel like when your spouse is depressed, angry or alienated? In this section you will learn how to project in your mind the visual imagery of your spouse's perceptions and feelings. This visual imagery is the basic foundation for all of the book's exercises and insights that together can lead to a blissful future for you and your spouse.

This section will teach you an important technique that I call merging. When we "merge" with our spouse we try to imagine how they are thinking and feeling by becoming one with them, mentally and emotionally. Merging does not mean invading another person's boundary to exert power and suppress them, but rather seeing and feeling the undercurrents in their thoughts and behavior in order to have more compassion for them. By merging with our spouse's feelings we can become attuned to their pain, joy and behavior. As you master this technique you will gain a deeper understanding and compassion — the compassion that brings permanent love.

First read this entire section, then close the book and do the visual imagery. Afterward, reopen the book and do Exercise 1, which follows in the next section.

Begin by finding a time and secluded place in your home with the least interruptions, telephones ringing, or other disturbing noises. Start this inner-mind observation into your spouse's past by closing your eyes and imagining that both of you are sitting in the same room, at a distance from each other, and watching a videotape of your spouse's childhood on a television screen. As your spouse's life story is unfolding before your eyes, his or her face lights up with a smile at the recollection of fond memories. Those memories represent the storeroom and the soul of childhood emotional life experiences.

As you watch that screen with your spouse, memories begin to surface from your own childhood. Remember that you are still observing your spouse watching the videotape.

Now for a moment I would like you to imagine sitting close to your spouse. Let's say you are holding your spouse in your arms so close that you hear their breath, smell and feel their skin. Now just imagine that the two of you begin to merge with each other until you are both of one mind in thoughts and feelings. You have in your possession your feelings and theirs, your memories and theirs, your joys and theirs, your pain and regrets and their pain and regrets. All the sensory perceptions become merged. Then, as you slowly move back to a distance, you will still be able to experience your spouse's feelings. Although you are now physically apart, you are still emotionally one with your spouse, merged by empathy and compassion.

As you continue to observe your spouse watching images from their childhood on the screen, you see your spouse's features become expressive: joy begins to relax their facial characteristics or raw pain deepens lines and wrinkles. Tears fill their eyes and roll down their cheeks. Their hands become tense and their shoulders sag. You suddenly touch your face and it is wet and your hands are tense because you have now merged with your spouse's feelings. On the screen a scene shows a happy and radiant young mother playing with her child, their voices bouncing with laughter. Now both your own and your spouse's features are softer and you laugh in unison with the image and feel the pleasure and joy. Both of you begin to remember such pleasant memories from your childhood, perhaps of playing or being pushed in a carriage by your mother, or being offered a treat.

Now suddenly other memories come back to you: you are dropped off at a caregiver's home when all you want is for your mother to be near you. Other scenes move rapidly in front of your eyes: you are alone while across the street three other children are playing together and you desperately want to join them. In another scene you are in class and the teacher has just humiliated you in front of all your classmates. As all those memories and feelings begin to resurface, you start thinking, "Wait a minute! This is too painful. I would rather concentrate on feeling good."

Unfortunately, those undesirable feelings are the sources of our adult life's discontent. These memories and experiences become repressed and cannot be wiped out. They remain, in a dormant cocoon stage, deep in each one of us. The memory will resurface again, triggered by an event or association, and will reawaken to bring pain in our lives and relationships. To avoid the pain of unpleasant memories, your brain may immediately serve you with a remembered pleasant image or you will fabricate one for yourself. That image may be genuine or fantasy. That good feeling will dull the pain for a short time, but the unpleasant memory may come back.

If you repress pain continuously, you will expend a great deal of energy to keep it down and avoid dealing with its meaning. Repression is a sure way to anesthetize pain, but one that presents danger. When we repress pain in our subconscious we become numb to feelings. Picture repression, if you will, as a walled fortress. Those walls prevent invaders from coming in but also stop you from going out. The walls will keep bad feelings out of your consciousness, but prevent you from experiencing good feelings. Painful memories, however, are like physical wounds: untreated, they fester.

By understanding our thoughts and feelings we can begin to understand others and what motivates behaviors. Each one of you will experience the same joyful and painful feelings. Therefore there is no dividing wall: it is not "him or me" or "her or me"; it is only "we" together and unified.

Threats, destructive behavior and conflicting beliefs in what constitutes marriage will be fueled by negative childhood experiences that govern our entire lives. The sooner we understand what lies beneath those past experiences, the sooner we can transform our lives into happy and blissful days where conflict is eliminated by examining and understanding its roots.

Exercise 1: Merging with My Spouse

Now open your journal and describe the experience of merging with your spouse. Explain how merging can help you better understand your spouse's feelings. Then condense the sentences into short statements. For example, if you wrote, "We both have similar painful and pleasant experiences from our past," condense it to: "We share similar feelings." Next, transfer those short statements to an index card and title it "Merging with My Spouse."

Conclusion

We feel our spouse's humanity, both pain and joy, by merging with them. We no longer see our spouse as the enemy. It is not "him or me" or "her or me"; it is only we together as one. We then erase the dividing line between two people and find the common bonds we all share. We temporarily reexamine our past to see what motivates our behavior. It is only when removing the masks we wear that we can uncover our true identity. We then take inventory and see how our past role-modeling can have an effect on our behavior now, and then move on to discover our real identity. The multi-generational emotional baggage we bring into the marriage must be discarded at the altar. The large amounts of energy we use to conceal ourselves can better be channeled into focusing on the real needs in our lives. Those needs can nourish and excite our marriage as we learn to share blissful moments with our spouse.

— 2 —

The First Years

The unconscious fear of abandonment is
what motivates control of another human being.

We had no clue, not the faintest idea of what marriage was all about when my husband and I married in 1960. All we knew was that we were in love and could not live without one another. We went our merry way into this unknown. We had no guidelines, except for what we had observed in our own families. We did not read a single book on marriage, nor did we have the wish to. Love would take care of us and everything else that came our way. Commitment, hardships, sacrifices, mutual understanding and respect would all fall into place.

Then as the first year elapsed, the increased demands and expectations of marriage stood in our way and all of our good intentions fell by the wayside. Marriage had become a battleground, and survival of the fittest came into play as all the emotional baggage we had brought into our marriage became stumbling blocks.

Three years later, as the proud parents of two children, although our differences were still unresolved we felt confident that we were quite capable of raising future adults and went about experimenting with childrearing. Good books on the subject were then available, but the thought never occurred to us to make use of them. A few years following that experimental period we acquired a lovely collie dog, and immediately ran out and bought a book on how to train a dog. But all through the years, we took for granted that marriage was "on-the-job training with no previous experience required." Fortunately, today information is available on how to avoid marital pitfalls by becoming informed about the latest discoveries on relationships and childrearing.

Control Issues

The first issues that come up in marriage in the early years are control issues. Controlling another human being is a survival tactic that we all acquire from infancy. It all starts with the control of your feeding and diaper-changing schedule as an infant. That cry escaping your hungry lips brought the anticipated response and you were fed or changed. By controlling your environment you gained the power to influence and command.

What is that "power trip" that drives human beings to fall into its grip? Exactly when and where does it begin? If you look back and remember the times when you felt powerful, what images come to mind? Perhaps it began when you were a small child and your caregiver understood your needs and responded quickly. You were then satisfied and felt secure that someone would always be there for you. During childhood, when your needs became expectations, you learned to depend on family members or friends to always be there, but painfully discovered that they disappointed you. You then began to feel forgotten or powerless.

Let's say, for example, that later on in school if you were rejected by a member of the opposite sex or you expected an "A" on an assignment and received only a "C" after trying your best, again you experienced this feeling of powerlessness. If no one then explained to you that disappointments and rejections do not necessarily have to repeat themselves infinitely, you may have internalized these experiences and used them as the basis for expected future outcomes. You felt that no matter what you tried, the outcome was out of your hands and beyond your power. These early childhood experiences can be the source of later power struggles.

A child subjugated by parental authority feels powerless and at the mercy of an authoritarian power. Later on, to regain a sense of power the child will transfer this external authority to an internal authority. In other words, the child's unconscious line of reasoning is: "I will appropriate your power and make it my own. I don't need you to exert your power upon me, I'd rather do it myself!" This is how children transfer criticism, abuse and authority to themselves by becoming their own tormentor and their own parental punisher. Thus begins a lifetime of perpetual self-recrimination, self-destructiveness (if the parents were abusive) and lack of self-regard. But now the young adult has power, the power of the parent within. Eventually that power becomes the wrong power and will undermine future growth.

In adulthood the sense of powerlessness that began in childhood resurfaces again. We then seek to take control of not only our life but our spouse's life. We are in charge. It becomes natural for us to want to control another because in our subconscious not to be in charge means to be powerless. This sense of powerlessness is often felt as in the past when we experienced it for the first time. Meanwhile, your spouse may also want to control you. She or he may be going through the same power struggle. Only the brain knows what it imprinted early in life. This blueprint remains there all the time and becomes triggered and active the minute we see the threat of powerlessness.

The irrational fear that giving power to our partner will make us as helpless as a child again can be terrifying and can prevent us from experiencing togetherness. Giving up our familiar ways of singlehood for a sharing way of life may also mean having to feel the pain of unresolved issues. Sometimes we stick to old ways that were safe, that have become our power, and hang on to old habits even though we may not remember why. Our "power habits" are the vestiges of childhood survival tactics for asserting ourselves and testing the world. In our brain we have imprinted how we can get power and how to exert that power to get the desired result.

The Brain's Blueprint

The brain is not only a marvelous and complex organ, it is also the last and greatest frontier (Carlson, 1995). To begin to understand the brain, we have to go back to childhood. The brain of a child from infancy to the age of ten—when new neuron multiply with their connections, or synapses— acquires a wealth of information that is processed continuously, becoming the blueprint that will remain with us for a lifetime. This blueprint for thought patterns is the basis and role model upon which we interpret our experiences later in life.

Our brain consists of many billions of neurons, and is thus able to work on different tasks at the same time. Our neuron connections, or synapses, regulate the flow of neurotransmitters (or as I call them, the "electric juices"), which take but a few milliseconds to transmit thought. Unlike a computer where information is programmed sequentially, our brain not only performs tasks simultaneously, but is also able to recognize a familiar face, remember a previous pleasant time with that person, and retrieve and verbally acknowledge the latest information that was stored about him. You may ask, "John, how are you? How did you resolve your business transaction the other day?" You have recognized the face by retrieving the information from your memory bank, but you also remembered what John was most recently dealing with in his work. This interaction with John took only milliseconds to process.

We retrieve information by association. Anything pertaining to John is stored, let's say, in John's "file" where there is a "John blueprint." That blueprint contains John's particulars such as his looks, his background, his job, etc. Next time you see John, he will impart some new bit of information about himself that you will store in his file. You will retrieve or remember information from his file instantly, if you see or think about him. It's as if the moment you think of John, a book opens up in front of your eyes and reveals pictures relating to him. The above, of course, are pleasant memories that you associate with John, so you welcome seeing him again. If the memories are not pleasant, however, you would feel uncomfortable or downright refuse to see him.

The Power Struggle over Needs

The blueprint for adult thought patterns begins to form in infancy. A hungry infant will cry to get the attention of the caregiver. As soon as that need is satisfied, the infant has stored the information on a blueprint that crying brings results. If the infant did not get immediate results, he will then try the next best thing: crying louder until he is satisfied. When there is still no satisfaction, he will get into a danger mode: holding his breath until he turns blue.

Hopefully the caregiver will have heard the cries of hunger pain. If not, this infant will then associate hunger pain with unmet needs.

Similarly, later in life when our needs are not satisfied, we may at first verbally communicate those needs and then get angry if results are not forthcoming, and ultimately we may become despondent if nothing works. Destructiveness and depression are reactions to unsatisfied needs that did not get attended to. Both destructiveness and depression work most of the time to attract attention and get results.

These early childhood experiences can be the source of power struggles later in life. If our caregiver knew our needs without us having to ask, we learned to expect the same from our partner or spouse. But waiting for our "parents" to fulfill our needs as adults is where we get into trouble.

The lines can become blurred when we superimpose our caregiver, mother or father, with our spouse. As children, getting our needs met was crucial for survival. Later in life we demand that our spouse satisfy our needs. But that spouse also has needs, and that is where expectations from both sides clash. Accusations fly: "If dinner was served on time, I wouldn't be snacking and then not be hungry when you finally served it!" And the impatient reply: "If you called me before you left work, I would've known when to put the steaks on!" When our need expectations are unfulfilled is when we hit the wall.

Let's face it, we get more training for a new job than we do for marriage. When we begin a new job we are trained to understand the needs of that particular position. Let's say the job is in sales. We ask the customers what they need or how we can help them. It's no different in a marriage or relationship. We court a partner and learn to discover their needs. The failure to attend to our partner's needs creates pain, and pain is what we tend to avoid by various methods: ignoring our partner, verbally abusing our partner, or just plain tuning out by isolating ourselves. It is when couples do not meet each other's needs that the power struggle begins.

In order not to feel helpless, we try to subjugate the other by means of control to force them to meet our needs; otherwise we feel they may abandon us. Control or power is a protection against fear of abandonment. Our fear of abandonment breeds this need to control the other. By limiting the other and making them feel powerless, we have gained control. Unfortunately, the powerless spouse will either actively reject this power control or resign themselves to it and turn to sickness or depression to attract attention. This need to control brings about the same result we tried to avoid in the first place: being abandoned by a spouse who will reject our control.

Merging With Your Spouse When Facing Conflict

Imagine for a moment that you had a perfect childhood: your mother and father were there and were satisfying your needs, and your life energy thrived. Now I would like you to go back to that room where you did the first merging imagery in Chapter 1 and again be the viewer. Your spouse is sitting in that chair surrounded by memories and you are watching, trying to feel their feelings, both their joys and their pain. In a rerun of the imagined videotape you see your spouse growing up, as if you were there in their childhood environment. You see the abuse your spouse was subjected to, the repression, all the unmet needs, the silencing of their voice, and the dehumanizing aspects of their childhood. What are your feelings toward your spouse now? If you said empathy, or a great surge of love impelling you to make it right for your spouse, I would say you are in the right ball park!

Now go back in time again to your own childhood memories. You can reexperience and feel the unhappy and painful times, just as your spouse did, only under different circumstances. The feelings evoked by the unpleasant or painful memories are the same that your spouse felt. You have now merged with your spouse, feeling the same emotions in experiencing painful childhood memories.

These, again, are only memories but the feelings are as strong as if they were happening today. Remember that all experiences are stored in the brain with their associated feelings. The memory of these past experiences triggers the feeling or pain that was stored along with them. A present experience can also trigger feelings from the past because of similar associations.

Whenever your partner reacts by being controlling or overbearing, balking, sulking, remaining silent or tuned out, it may very well be that your spouse has suddenly returned to that painful childhood. Your partner's behavior could be caused by the triggering effect of a past association, a word, insult or humiliating remark you may have said. When your spouse is acting in an impatient, rude or destructive manner, it is because of pain. The pain and fear underneath is the motivating force behind the negative behavior.

Learn to merge with your partner whenever he or she is experiencing these feelings, and try to mirror their pain by feeling compassion—the same kind of compassion you might feel for a stranger in a newspaper story who has experienced a heartbreaking loss. This is not to say that whenever your spouse is going through a painful recollection triggered by your need, you have to bypass that need. Merging is only a method for better understanding your spouse when conflicts arise, and for overcoming your reluctance to give in to your spouse's demands.

❧ ❧ ❧

A Case Study

Usually when conflicts arise between spouses, it is because they were each accustomed to a different set of rules when growing up. For example, a couple who we shall call Mike and Katie came from opposite backgrounds. Mike was raised as an only child and had most of his needs attended to as he was growing up, and his life took a fairly average course. Katie grew up in a large family with three brothers and two sisters and had to live with less attention to her needs. Katie always fantasized as a young girl about meeting her handsome prince who would see that her needs always came first. This wish had been very strong in her life, and when she met Mike she was swept off her feet by his attention and willingness to please her in every detail during their courtship.

Now years later, and three children into the marriage, Katie's main complaint about Mike is that he neglects her needs and often ignores her requests for more attention. For Mike to satisfy Katie's needs, he has to forgo the habit of being the first attended to as he was while growing up.

❧ ❧ ❧

Frequently when conflict takes place between two people who are still much in love and who want to continue their relationship, it is because of their past experiences and how their expectations were integrated into their psyches. It is important to remember when conflict occurs to stop and evaluate why your spouse is demanding and expecting you to fulfill his or her request. In most instances every expectation has its root in the past. In Katie's case, her discontent is not only that Mike fails to acknowledge her needs, but that Katie's childhood went unfulfilled.

Exercise 2: Understanding My Partner's Requests

First write down in your journal instances where you asked your spouse to do something for you, and your spouse was reluctant to fulfill your request. Then ask your spouse, gently, if anything in his or her childhood was similar to a recent request you made, and why your spouse resisted granting it. You can ask these questions with the understanding that your spouse may feel reluctant at first to discuss these matters with you. Your spouse may also take your questioning as personal criticism. Briefly explain why you are asking these questions to dispel any misunderstanding.

Next write down what your spouse expects from you, and ask yourself how your resistance to fulfilling those requests relates to your childhood.

It is only when we understand our spouse or partner that we can merge with that significant other in our life and become a harmonious couple, the Yin and the Yang, becoming one and regaining wholeness. By fulfilling your partner's needs, you have sown the seeds for the gratefulness and love that will rebound and come back to you to make you whole again.

Conclusion

The fear of abandonment is what drives us to control another human being. Repeated disappointments in our life can lead to a feeling of powerlessness, and our wish to control events and people around us can give us the wrong kind of power. Our brain retains the original blueprint pattern that will guide us through a lifetime. If our needs are not satisfied, we draw attention to ourselves through destructiveness, despondency or depression. We have to discover our spouse's needs. It is only when we give attention to our partner's needs that our needs will be satisfied. When conflicts arise, try to merge with your partner and feel their pain or past losses.

The Difficult Years

All, everything that I understand,
I understand only because I love.

—Leo Tolstoy

Most couples say that the most difficult years in their marriage occurred between the first and seventh year. Those early years are the testing period on who will control the marriage and who will be controlled. Other couples say that their most difficult years were when their children had left the nest and the couple was faced with all their unresolved issues that had been put on the back burner for the kids' sake or swept under the carpet. In those cases the carpet covered a thick layer of dust that escaped from time to time, recharging the atmosphere with conflicts.

No issue can remain locked away forever. The energy expended in suppressing it can jeopardize the entire marriage or relationship. The answer is to face and try to solve issues and conflicts right away. From the start, a marriage may be subjected to: control issues, family influences, illnesses, financial woes, unemployment, alienation, regrets, or verbal, emotional, sexual or physical abuse. With all these roadblocks it is a miracle that marriages survive at all! Of course, the statistics are irrefutable: by the 1990s the rate of divorce had tripled since the 1960 census. In 1994, 1.2 million divorces were granted, and it is estimated that "nearly half of all new marriages will end in divorce" (*Los Angeles Times*, 1998). Furthermore, children of divorce have higher odds of becoming high school dropouts, getting hooked on drugs and becoming pregnant (*Los Angeles Times*, 1996).

The toll on the divorced adults is immeasurable. First there are poorer financial conditions for both partners; the divorced husband gets saddled with alimony, and the ex-wife has to work outside the home to support herself while taking care of the children and her household at the same time. The bitterness, acrimony and arguments between the divorced partners create an atmosphere of resentment for the children. In addition, divorce may be a reenactment of the couple's own parents' divorce. The cycle of divorce is unending and creates more and new dysfunctions in the family and in future generations. Divorce also teaches a child that problems can only be resolved by fleeing the nest.

What is the solution then? How can we break out of this vicious cycle and bring order and harmony into our lives? The answer to those questions is to revamp our way of thinking while keeping in mind the source of our happiness and bliss: viewing our spouses as ourselves. We then go back to Chapter 1 of this book when we merged with our partner's private thoughts and upbringing.

Reenacting the Past

If your partner came from a divorced family, the odds are that he or she will reenact the tensions, strife and arguments in their family of origin. You might say, "Why on earth would anyone want the same thing to happen to them? Wouldn't they try everything in their power to prevent it?" Perhaps, but children of divorce will subconsciously tend to think of themselves as unworthy of being loved or of having a successful marriage. They fall into the same pattern—or pit, so to speak—without consciously being aware of it. Another factor that helps explain why they might reenact their parents' divorce is role-modeling. Think of living in a family where the parents are distant, alienated or distrustful. Children growing up in this atmosphere will learn, "or imprint," that this is the norm. Having no other model to refer to, they will subconsciously choose the one they experienced. How would anyone know the right approach to marriage unless it was experienced?

When you observed your partner in the visualization exercise in Chapter 1, you saw their childhood in your mind's eyes. You saw and experienced their disappointments in life, like your disappointments in life. You saw their rejection by parents, peers or society, just like the rejections you experienced while growing up. You felt their sadness, sighs and tears as they viewed their lives in slow motion, and felt one with them. You felt their being as your being. Even if your partner did not come from a divorced family, he or she nonetheless experienced a lack of fulfillment of their needs if their parents were unhappy themselves. Remember that if your parents were unfulfilled in their lives, they could not fully attend to your needs for affection or attention. This is where the cycle of unhappiness was handed down to your generation, and you will hand it down to your children, and they in turn will do the same to their children, your grandchildren.

No matter how your parents rationalize that they provided amply for your needs and did the best they could, there will always be a certain need that went unfulfilled. That is, if your father or mother was unhappy, you will subconsciously feel responsible for it and occupy most of your life in making up for their unhappiness. Meanwhile your spouse will feel your alienation, and your children will repeat the cycle all over again.

How can we solve this dilemma for our unhappy parents? We cannot. We only have one life to live and that is our own. That's not to say that our parents do not deserve our sympathy for their failed lives. All you can do is understand their pain, and attend to some of their needs while leaving room for your own life. Remember that mental energy is not infinite. The more we think of our parents' failed or miserable lives, the more we take time away from our own lives. It is not selfish in the least to focus only on your life the majority of the time. The solution then is to strike a happy medium.

It is important to remember that you are not responsible for your parents' failed lives. This, by the way, reminds me of the unhappy teenager shouting at their father or mother the familiar phrase: "I didn't ask to be born!" This is understandable. If we could ask the unborn how they want their life to be, we would solve all ills. They would have, for example, a long list of wants: "I want good parents. I want you to love each other. I want you to be happy so I can be happy and not have to think about how to make you happy. I want laughter. I want to be proud of my parents. I want to tell my future children how my parents stood by me in good times and bad times. I want, I want, I want, etc." This list could go on forever for there is no end to happiness. Happiness breeds more happiness in an unending cycle.

Exercise 3: How to Be in Love

In your journal write down a list of *happy wants or needs* you strongly desire. You can include in this list health, love, affection, or attention. Then transfer these desires, and how to achieve them, to an index card. For example, you may write : "I want more affection from my husband [or wife]." Then underneath that line you might list: a) "I will pay more attention when he [or she] is talking to me"; b) "I will hold his [or her] hand anywhere or anytime"; c) "I will plant little kisses on his [or her] neck, hand, arm, etc."

You will experience an amazing return of affection as soon as you act upon this list—or as soon as the ice is broken, and your spouse has recovered from shock if he or she has been love-starved for a long time. As a French saying says, "L'appetit vient en mangeant," meaning "Appetite comes as one eats," or love comes as one loves. This card is to be kept with you always. Title this card "How to Be in Love."

Example of a Needs List

My Needs	My Partner's Needs
I need more affection.	I need more attention when I'm speaking.
I need more loving sex.	I need more passion in lovemaking.
I need more closeness.	I need more time together.
I need more understanding of my needs.	I need some space to feel a longing for you.

Exercise 4: How to Fulfill My Partner's Needs

On another index card, list what your spouse's needs are. Yes, you will mentally do their exercise as well and put down the needs they may have expressed to you in the past. If you cannot remember, you can ask, "What are your needs now in our marriage or relationship and what can I do to help?" The benefits will be twofold if your questions motivate your spouse to draw up their own needs list. Title this card "How to Fulfill My Partner's Needs."

Resolving Conflicts

When your spouse or partner has brought to your attention an unsatisfied need or a dilemma, try to help them work on it immediately. I know that our lives are kept so busy with work, children, friends and obligations that we forget to set time aside for ourselves and our partners.

In some families, conflicts are discussed at the dinner table. That can give you indigestion, and you are liable to get cross with each other. Food should preferably be consumed in a quiet atmosphere with pleasant music in the background and with your energies focused on the food itself and your taste buds. Non-controversial subjects can be discussed at the table in a quiet voice without trying to subdue one another in an atmosphere of control. The best time for discussing family or spousal issues is after dinner or perhaps earlier in the morning while having a cup of coffee together in bed. When needs are attended to right away, they are put to rest and do not consume precious energy we need to perform tasks such as driving to work, working or attending a meeting. Nothing is more distracting than having pressing needs ignored.

In conflict resolution we have to reveal ourselves to each other. In revealing our innermost feelings, we may express anxiousness, discomfort or pain. It is not a sign of weakness to show that we are hurting, it is a sign of strength. We all have been wounded as children and when conflict occurs it reactivates these wounds. When we argue and feel wounded, we automatically go into a defense mode. We need to remind ourselves that the issue or argument being discussed at the moment is separate from the past. This is when we recover our adult voice and discuss the matter rationally. We can say, "I'd prefer that you didn't use those words; it reminds me of when I was a child ..." Your partner will understand immediately. But if your partner persists in their anger, you can ask, "I see that you are hurt. Can you think of an incident in your past that I have reactivated by my actions or my words?" Your question should be asked in a calm voice if possible. There is nothing worse than shouting it as an accusation.

Paraphrase your partner's answer, statement or request. For example, if their complaint is, "We don't spend enough time together," you can say, "If I understand you correctly, you feel lonely and would like more time with me. If you like, we can spend time together every morning before we leave for work, okay?" or "How about reading to each other an hour every night, or listening to music?" Again, your attitude, quickness and willingness to understand will depend on how fulfilled you are within yourself.

When resolving conflicts and differences of opinion, make a mental list of why you dislike what you are hearing from your partner. Besides the possibility that you reactivated past hurts, perhaps you may have misunderstood your partner's message. Look into your own thinking and ask yourself, "Why is it that this comment bothers me so much? Why do I feel ruffled, rejected or stampeded upon?" Quite often what we think of ourselves will color our perceptions. Be honest with yourself and ask, for example, "If I feel rejected, does this mean that everyone rejects me or that everyone has to love me?" Or perhaps you think, "I cannot fail, or it would kill me." Many times this kind of reasoning will keep you from communicating clearly with your partner and put you in an automatic self-defense mode, which does not solve arguments. Self-defense has the effect of a shield that will deflect your partner's argument and catapult it back like a boomerang.

How then are you to think clearly without going into self-defense or war mode? The first thing to do is to ask yourself a list of questions and answer them honestly. You have to look at a specific situation or argument and ask, for example, "Why do I feel rejected when my partner does not respond to me right away?" The answer is the irrational beliefs that we acquired while growing up: "I am rejected because I am not loved," or "I get anxious because I don't know if I'll be noticed." This feeling of rejection, or of being invisible, is firmly rooted in the belief of not being loved. In other words, if the outcome (not being loved) is blamed on a specific event, it is an irrational belief. It is the belief that caused the outcome. Your belief of being rejected caused you hurt feelings. It is not because your partner said one thing or another or refused to accommodate you immediately. Irrational beliefs are deeply rooted in our psyche due to conditioning while growing up. If you disobeyed your parents and were punished without explanation, you automatically felt unloved or that they loved your brother or sister more.

Many times our way of thinking is what causes hurt feelings, and that can become a source of conflicts. There are many irrational beliefs that control our thinking and cause us to act in a certain way out of fear. Below are some of the fears caused by our irrational beliefs.

Fear of rejection: *I must be loved all the time.*

Fear of failure: *I can't fail; I must be perfect.*

Fear of unfairness: *Everybody has to be fair to me.*

Fear of facing issues: *If I don't talk about it, it will be forgotten.*

Fear of punishment: *If something bad happened, then it must be my fault or I must make myself miserable.*

These are some of the irrational beliefs we have due to our past conditioning. However, this past conditioning need not become an excuse for us to avoid facing the issues, as uncomfortable as they may make us. By sifting through irrational beliefs in ourselves and others, we can begin to see clearly and make rational decisions.

Irrational Thoughts and Beliefs

Situation	Emotion	Irrational Thought/Belief
Childhood: My father is angry at me.	I'm scared.	He doesn't love me. (Irr. thought) Therefore I'm no good. (Irr. belief)
Adulthood: I feel neglected.	I'm lonely and scared.	He/she doesn't love me. (Irr. Thought) Therefore he/she loves someone else. (Irr. belief)

These irrational thoughts and beliefs follow each other interchangeably. If the belief is "I'm no good," the irrational thought that will follow is "I'm not lovable."

Exercise 5: Eliminating Irrational Thoughts and Beliefs

Now turn to your journal and write down as many irrational thoughts and beliefs you think you may have. The way to identify them is to examine bad feelings you have now or had in the past and work back to what you think caused you to feel that way. Then take an index card and list those irrational thoughts and beliefs. Underneath each one, write a rational explanation. If you wrote down, for example: "It's my fault that my parents' divorce happened," then underneath it you might write, "I had no control over my parents' decision to divorce." Title this card "Eliminating Irrational Thoughts and Beliefs."

By examining the reasons behind certain behaviors or words, you have the power to determine whether you want to end a conflict or perpetuate it. You can ask yourself many questions such as "Why do I want to solve this issue?" or "Why was I so angry when she or he said that to me?" or "How can I precisely convey my thoughts or feelings to my partner?"

Above all, try to listen to your partner without interrupting or going into a self-defense mode. Many times we become distracted thinking about what we are going to say next instead of hearing what the other person is saying. It is extremely frustrating when a listener looks away while you are talking to them. Watch for those behaviors in yourself and in your partner.

Listening and being silently present is the first step in actively resolving conflicts. Paraphrasing your partner's message is extremely gratifying—now your partner knows you are really listening. These techniques can enhance conflict resolution and bring harmony into your life.

Listening to Needs to Resolve Issues

1. **Listen**	Focus on the speaker's eyes or mouth if your thoughts tend to wander.
2. **Don't interrupt**	Your partner may lose their train of thought, increasing their frustration.
3. **Paraphrase**	Repeat in your own words what your partner said to you.
4. **Reply**	What are you going to say to help fulfill their need?

Exercise Progress

By now you have worked on Exercises 1 through 5 and spent at least five to ten minutes each day practicing. Go back if you did not do those exercises so that you may build upon them.

Conclusion

One of the keys to a *blissful marriage* is to *resolve conflicts* as soon as possible. Use *merging, introspection* and ask *questions* to clear the impasse in your marriage. We do not live our parents' lives. We can only *live our lives*. You are not responsible for your parents' failed lives. *Happiness* breeds more *happiness*. Past hurts can reactivate pain and cause us to defend ourselves over unrelated issues in the present. The *irrational beliefs* we have of ourselves can color our perceptions and put us into an automatic self-defense mode. By rejecting past irrational beliefs about ourselves or others, we can *focus* on solving the present issue. That is when we can make *rational decisions*. The time we spend with our partner or spouse is *sacred*.

— 4 —

The Extended Family:

Expectations and the Roles We Play

What happens to a dream deferred?
Does it dry up like a raisin in the sun?
Or fester like a sore—And then run?
Does it stink like rotten meat?
Or crust and sugar over—Like a syrupy sweet?
Maybe it just sags like a heavy load.
Or does it explode?

—Langston Hughes

Children have the capacity to learn and absorb everything they see all around them. At the same time, they possess the unique ability to reach their own conclusions. If children are abused, they will learn that they are not important enough to be loved by the adult caregiver or parent and that adults are not to be trusted. For when we trust someone, we know that we can love or regard them without constraint. The moment they betray our trust, we listen or do things for them with reluctance and learn to be forever on our guard.

Family Influences

How often did you hear your mother or father wishing that you would pursue a specific career when you were growing up? When you finally selected a profession suited to your own goals in life, they could not understand what in the world possessed you to select that particular one. Your parents' ideas of what profession suited you may have been a transference of what they had wanted for themselves. The wish to procreate is to project our being and desires onto our children and therefore live through them forever.

But as the poet and prophet Kahlil Gibran said: "Your children are not your children. They come through you not from you. And though they are with you yet they belong not to you." We are not our parents' property nor are we in this world to fulfill their wishes and desires for their lives. Their influence can make us forget who we are and dutifully follow their advice or wishes. The family bond we share with them forces us to obey with reluctance.

We must ask ourselves, are we sheep or individuals with our own wishes and desires? How much influence should we let others have over us? To what extent can we draw the line between someone's well-meaning advice and their forceful control over our lives? These are all conflicting thoughts that can split our psyche or individuality and cause chaos in our mind.

When we were growing up, we did as we were told because we had no way of fending for ourselves. Now, however, as adults we can provide for ourselves, and if we are dissatisfied with our lot, we need to rethink our original goals and wishes that we had growing up. We need to recapture that fresh and young essence that we possessed in the beginning.

Now go back in time and try to remember all the wishes you had. See them in their realistic context. You may have wished to be an astronaut and go to the moon or become President of the United States. Not that it's unrealistic to achieve these two professions, but if much time has passed, thinking or reminiscing will not do. It will not get you far unless perhaps you are still in your twenties or thirties and have had access to the professions leading to those careers. True, there is such a thing as "never too late." Some vocations, however, may fall into the "too late" category for you. In that case, the only thing dissatisfied reminiscing will do is rob you of vital energy that could be focused on better things such as your present relationship with your spouse.

Exercise 6: Career Possibilities

Now turn to your journal and write down all the careers you have dreamt of as far back as you can remember. Then number them in a list in order of importance. When you're finished, cross out the ones that are impossible to achieve in your lifetime and circle those that may have a remote possibility. Then go through the ones circled and ask yourself, what are the realistic possibilities that you could achieve them in your lifetime? Be fair with yourself and don't close the door on any unless they would be financially ruinous. If so, cross them out.

By now you may have two or three careers that might be realistic. Take an index card and write them down in order of importance. On the back of this card write how and when you can begin to realize these dreams. Keep this card accessible to remind you of what you can still achieve in your lifetime. Review this card periodically if you are dissatisfied in your present job or career. This card, however, is not to be used when conditions at work can be remedied or conflicts resolved. Now put this book aside and do the exercise. Title this card "Career Possibilities."

Missed Opportunities

Go back now to those thoughts of missed opportunities before you did Exercise 6. Think back to your regrets at not having realized these opportunities. Remember how often you thought about it and how it put you in a painful state of mind if the regret was overwhelming. Now I want you to go back to your parents', grandparents' or uncles' and aunts' wishes if they were significant in your life. Did they impart to you how they missed opportunities in their lives? Did they suggest what path you should take when you grew up?

As your relatives' wishes for themselves fell by the wayside, they tried to live their dreams through you or your children. You can now merge with them and feel their regrets and unfulfilled lives and see how they influenced your approach to life, career or childrearing. Quite often I hear about the mother-in-law cliché or the domineering father or mother keeping their children under their control. These domineering but significant people in your life are beings who were once thriving, wishing and hoping to achieve great things in their own lives. When those dreams never happened, your parents' hopes may have become a holy grail to pursue through you and your achievement of those dreams.

Throughout your impressionable young life, your parents' frustrations with careers, making ends meet, or other obstacles in their lives became the source of your life discontent that trapped you in a vicious cycle. Keep this in mind as you gently remind them that it is your life and your decision to veer away to forge a new career. Many times in life we are influenced by our parents' inability to achieve their dreams. We model ourselves upon them, and often cannot surpass them because of a subconscious feeling of guilt or loyalty.

Ask yourself, how has this cycle of unfulfilled goals in your parents' lives and in your own life affected your present relationship? Is there a pattern where a deep dissatisfaction with your job affects your mood? When you come home from work, what are the thoughts that dominate your behavior toward your spouse, children or other loved ones? Of course, with today's commutes, even if you like your job and leave fairly satisfied at the end of the day, the drive home can turn you into a wreck.

Exercise 7: The Influences on My Career

Turn again to your journal and write down a list of career influences that you were exposed to both growing up and as an adult. For example:

Career Influences in My Life

1. Parents' influence - The profession they wished I would pursue.

2. Spouse's influence - The profession my spouse wanted, or still wants for me.

3. Society's influence - The professions with more money, status, glamour, or appeal.

4. My own influence - The professions I would wish for family, friends, etc.

On an index card write down the career influences that came the closest to your own aspirations but were never achieved. Now look at what you wrote down and add how you might make them realistic career possibilities. Keep this card also accessible. Title this card "The Influences on My Career."

This exercise does not mean that you should quit your job if it is presently satisfying and has sensible earnings, unless to do so would not jeopardize that security. The exercise is intended to put into focus the repressed wishes buried inside you for so long. Your vital energy that is used to repress those wishes can best be focused on your marriage. Remember that you are the product of your parents, peers and society. To break the bonds requires a great amount of energy, patience and understanding on your part. It is only when you have compassion for your parents' missed opportunities in life that you can have compassion for your own lost chances. You now share those lost dreams, except that you still have the opportunity to change your life. When you reach your dream, you can later impart to your children how you reached your vision. They in turn will know that if this vision became true for you, then it is also possible for them.

Conclusion

Trust brings safety and love. Without this trust we learn to have no self-regard and to always be on our guard. *We are not sheep.* We are *individuals* with our *own wishes* and *desires*. We need to *rediscover* who we are and our *original goals* in life. Eliminate *unrealistic expectations* of yourself and others. *Merge* with your parents and close relatives to see how their dreams or regrets have influenced your career aspirations or goals in life. *Unleash* those repressed wishes and put them into perspective as realistic goals. *Communicate* to your next generation how your realistic *vision* has activated your new future.

— 5 —

When Is It Enough?

---

*I have grown tired of sorrow and human tears: life is a
dream in the night, a fear among fears, a naked runner
lost in a storm of spears.*

—Arthur Symons

When do you know you have had enough of conflict,
bitterness and misery? Many of us do not know when
it is enough even as we go on suffering and sinking into a
paralysis of will. We fight, sulk, make up, then go on
repeatedly.

Does it mean then that in marriage we have no
disagreements? Of course we do. We can disagree on
various points: management of money, raising children, or
allowable behavior. Arguing is one thing, but recurring and
escalating fighting on the same issues is another. This more
serious fighting occurs when all else has failed. Your partner
has developed deaf ears to your requests and will not budge
because of some unrealistic idea she or he has of
partnership.

Standstills in marriage can be caused by numerous
factors that were fostered by upbringing and early
role-modeling: a breakdown in communication, unfulfilled
needs, physical or emotional abuse, neglect or withholding

love and affection, a love-and-hate relationship, family reenactments, family influences and illness. We will examine each of these reasons in detail in this chapter.

When one or both spouses feel they have had enough of their marriage and want to chuck it at the divorce court, they need to stop and examine the situation carefully. Before reaching for the divorce papers it is wise to look within and see where each has veered from the intended path. We need to see our human frailty and vulnerability as well as our partner's, examine our attitudes toward our partner, then look for ways to breach the abyss.

Breakdown in Communication

The first thing you need to discover when there is strife in marriage is why the breakdown in communication occurred. For some reason unknown to us, we become obstinate and object to having a constructive dialogue. For example, the only dialogue existing in a blocked marriage is: "What's for dinner?" or "Did you pick up my clothes at the cleaners?" or "Why are the kids playing in the mud?" or "Did you talk to your boss about a raise?" or "Why can't we take a vacation?"

It's not that these are unreasonable questions in marital dialogues. The problem is that the questions get answered in the same monotonous tone of voice with no warmth added to the communication. The replies might be of the sort: "Can't you tell by the smell?" or "Pick up your own cleaning!" or "Don't bother me about the kids!" or "I told you not to nag me about that raise!" or "I don't want to talk about a vacation now." This type of communication puts an immediate damper on dialogue and discourages the other partner from pursuing a conversation.

If stones could talk they would sound like these exchanges between this husband and wife. These two individuals have left their emotions and feelings bottled up. Usually when that happens, each spouse has built a protective wall against hurt and pain. Sometimes the pain is so great that to address it would bring on a tide of rage and anger against each other. This controlled tide has accumulated from successive demands and needs that were not met. In the long run each spouse will retreat into their fort of impenetrable walls, which keep the pain in and prevent the healthy expression of love, affection and warmth.

Examples of a Caring and Warm Communication Exchange

Request	Reply
What's for dinner?	You'll love what I cooked today.
Did you pick up my clothes at the cleaners?	Sorry, honey, I forgot all about it.
Why are the kids playing in the mud?	I told them it's okay before their baths.
Did you talk to your boss about a raise?	I lost my courage at the last minute.
Why can't we take a vacation?	It bothers me that we can't afford it right now.

In each reply, the one answering puts forward their emotions and feelings without fear of reprisal from the other spouse. Granted, this should be the ideal dialogue when there is no fear that the other spouse will strike back with criticism or a bullying attitude that conceals power or manipulation. Many times when we express our disappointments and frustration we fear being labeled weak. The society in which we grew up stressed strength as a shield against all attitudes and emotions, and more so for men than for women. But expressing our fear and feelings to our partner will show our vulnerability and encourage our partner to respond in kind. When one spouse reveals his or her deep emotions and fears, it then leads to opening a door to merging and understanding. In addition, it keeps the road open for further communication.

Unfulfilled Needs

Unfulfilled needs are major reasons for leaving one's spouse to begin the search for another. Those denied needs can be anything from not being heard to having love and sex withheld by the other spouse. There could be many reasons for turning a deaf ear to a spouse, such as not wanting to face issues and problems. But problems are usually resolved by a two-way communication, allowing room for compromise and a workable solution. When one partner does not want resolution, it could mean that he or she: 1) is afraid of change, since the problem is at least familiar, 2) is afraid of opening a Pandora's box to other problems and now having two instead of one, or 3) is suddenly overwhelmed.

Withholding love and sex from the other spouse is a deep problem that demands every attention, including seeing a sex therapist to unravel the dilemma. The first thing the sexually frustrated partner needs to do is confront the issue head-on but without relentlessness. Sexual needs are vital to both partners' health and peace of mind. A lack of sex could stem from ignoring a partner's wishes in love making, satisfying only oneself without seeing to the other partner's satisfaction, holding rage against a partner, being turned off because of other unfulfilled issues, and most common, satisfying another outside the marriage as in infidelity. Sometimes unfulfilled sexual needs can bring on other problems, and vice versa: other problems can cause a lack of sex.

Many times unfulfilled needs can be brought on by outside factors such as the demands of a frustrating job, being stymied by a lack of education and professional advancement, or financial deadlock. When these occur, the life goes out of living and loving while the other spouse becomes the brunt or outlet for the frustrating dilemma. Usually this situation is the result of transference, where one is unable to resolve their issue with the right source and instead transfers all their frustration to their spouse. It's sort of like "passing the buck" except that this "buck" is loaded with anger, resentment and punishment for the other spouse. Through communication, one spouse has the responsibility to uncover what's troubling the other before it becomes unmanageable. It behooves the other spouse to become the "detective spouse."

Uncovering and Resolving Unfulfilled Needs

Frustrated Spouse	Detective Spouse
I had a miserable day today at work.	What happened, honey? Tell me.
I don't want to talk about it.	Perhaps after dinner you'll feel better.
Perhaps.	Let's eat, then talk.

In this exchange, one spouse encouraged the other to talk but wisely suggested a talk after dinner when their stomachs are full and both are more relaxed. This approach opens the door for communication, and reestablishes a homeostasis and balance in the marriage. A working marriage is like a seesaw: when one spouse is down the other has to find the strength to be up. If both partners are constantly down it's a losing marriage.

Abuse in Marriage

Abuse is a serious breach in the marriage. It means that the partnership is unequal with one partner exerting power over the other. Abuse can take many forms — addictions such as alcoholism, gambling and infidelity, emotional abuse (withholding love, affection or sex) to total rejection of the other partner or physical harm. Again, the other partner has to uncover the reasons for the behavior and bring about a resolution through marriage counseling or confronting the abusing spouse to face their problem. In abuse, the abused partner has to resist the tendency to think and feel that he or she is unloved, and must gather their strength to fight the crisis head-on.

Physical abuse can be dangerous and life threatening. In physical abuse, the first thing abused partners must do is protect themselves against injury from the abuser; if they possibly can. The next step is to find a calm period and begin an investigation, so to speak, to find out what caused the physical abuse. The resolution is clear in physical abuse: either the abuser ceases immediately or the right authority is required to step in. Physical abusers are most often repeat offenders and no compromise is acceptable. Immediate attention is warranted in resolving the problem, as well as counseling by a professional in the field.

Non-physical abuse, such as emotional abuse, where one partner withholds love or affection from the other partner, is hard to detect. Abused partners will automatically feel they are unloved, especially if they had experienced the same abuse in childhood. In this case the abused partner will retreat into their pain and will not fight back. In order to filter out the reasons behind the lack of affection the abused partner has to confront the emotional abuser. It takes great determination and strength to learn the real reasons for his or her isolation.

Emotional abuse takes an immeasurable toll on the abused partner. The abuse can range from withdrawing love and affection, to verbally brow beating a partner and making them feel inadequate, inefficient thereby stripping them of their self-esteem. The abused partner will be anxiety ridden with the constant nagging fear of being wrong in suspecting the other partner. Most damaging for the abused partner is the conflict of having to leave a spouse they still love emotionally.

A Case Study

Mike and Judy's first two years of marriage is now full of arguing and fighting. Judy cannot understand Mike's sudden behavior change. He had become rude and verbally abusive toward her, and exploded at the slightest remark or question. Mike also came home late at night and gave inexplicable reasons for his absences. Judy felt ridden with anxieties and suspected that Mike was having an affair.

Confronting an Emotionally Abusive Partner

Abused Partner	Abusive Partner
Judy: Mike, why are you always so late?	*Mike:* Don't nag me!

Abused Partner	Abusive Partner
Judy: (facing him) Are you having an affair?	*Mike*: (raising his voice) You're barking up the wrong tree!
Judy: (on the verge of tears) Wrong tree or not, I have to know!	*Mike*: (now yelling) There is nothing going on!
Judy: Either you tell me or I'm leaving!	*Mike*: (smirking) You can't manage on your own.
Judy: I can manage very well without you!	Mike: Go! See if I care!

Love-and-Hate Relationship

A love-and-hate relationship in a marriage is a no-win relationship. It's like trying to fill a glass that has a small hole at the bottom. The two partners might be in an upbeat mood, then at the slightest provocation they erupt into arguments and fights. This situation usually involves an enmeshed marriage where the partners have no boundaries and each one imposes their will upon the other.

For example, Marie and Daniel have always given the appearance of a loving and devoted couple. Marie served Daniel's meals on time, was responsible for overseeing his vitamin intake, set Daniel's wardrobe in impeccable order and was also a sexual partner to him with devotion. If Daniel made a slight mistake she would blast at him, reprimand him over and over until he had to cover his ears, then withhold sex from him as punishment. Marie had a history of physical abuse as a child and at the slightest provocation she would turn against her partner as if he were the adversary. Marie's rage was ready to pop up at any moment, even when uncalled for.

Other examples of enmeshed relationships include relatives such as parents, uncles or aunts who monetarily support children, nieces or nephews, then dictate their will upon those members of the family. The children then become prisoners of their will like fish caught in a net or mesh. An enmeshed relationship needs space and the recognition that no partner can impose their will upon another. A partnership in marriage means just that: two partners sharing equally in the benefits and pooling their resources for the good of both in that union.

Repeated strife that has eroded the foundation in a marriage has a ripple effect on the children. The children's loyalty in that marriage gets caught in a tug-of-war between the parents no matter how much attention they get from either parent. This occurs because children see things as whole. Children cannot understand split love, split affection, or split loyalty. That is exactly what happens, however, in divorce and disharmony in the home. When Dad divorces Mom he also divorces his children. That is how a child internalizes the divorce: If Dad cannot love Mom, then he cannot love me or may stop loving me too later. This lack of love is perceived on a subconscious level and the fear of it is always lurking in the background. On the surface, of course, the child knows that Dad and Mom will do their utmost to stand by them and support them, but on a deeper level the child will feel unloved and rejected.

A divorce usually means that problems in the marriage were never solved and were allowed to fester beyond repair. A problem that is not solved within a reasonable amount of time will breed other problems such as resentment, anger, rage, loss of love and affection, and become so muddy that to unravel who did what to whom becomes an impossible task. Before a marriage reaches that stage, the partners need to see a warning light. That light will alert them that they have gone far enough in imposing their will upon the other and they need to sit down and iron out the disagreements.

I knew a couple who used a method of flashing a red light when one partner or the other became out of control, transferred aggression from work onto their spouse, raised their voice or became stubborn in their view or opinion. They both had agreed beforehand to use that method to alert the other partner when they were running into trouble. Today, that couple uses that method sparingly and both are extremely grateful to each other for cooperating in a loving partnership.

Family Reenactments

Family-of-origin reenactment is a major contributor to attitudes, behavior and future outcomes in the marriage. Family attitudes and behavior are usually brought into the marriage and perpetuated without the partners noticing that they are unloading dead weight baggage into the relationship. For example, a father's infidelity can influence his son to follow in his footsteps. The son may shun the behavior at first and castigate his father for it, but later in life, at the slightest provocation by his spouse, he may use this outlet and commit adultery himself. He may rationalize his behavior along the lines of "she led me to it," or "I have the right to be happy," or the rift caused between the partners will be used as an excuse. But in this instance the adultery is an internalization of the father's behavior: "What is good for my father is good for me too." Society also does not help in this matter. A young male's entire life is permeated with modeled, ingrained behavior of other males straying from the marriage. The unspoken understanding among "the boys" is that straying is acceptable behavior to be dismissed with a smile and a wink. Meanwhile, the children in such marriages sense a problem and are saddened by Mom's sadness.

Other reenactments of family life include the way parents treated each other, from the henpecked father and resentful mother looking for partnership and male authority in the home, to the domineering father using violence to subdue others to his will. "I remember growing up and being afraid when Dad got mad. We were all silent as mice," said one man who sought therapy after his wife and grown children refused to speak to him until he toned down his violent outbursts. Violence and destructive behavior are means to impose one's will upon an unsuspecting partner. By showing anger or rage the message is: "You do what I want or else!" The unsuspecting partner will search high and low in their mind for what caused the outburst or how they contributed to it. In many instances, the wronged partner will blame themselves: "He (or she) does not love me," or "I am not attractive, young or good-looking enough," or "Someone else looks better." This tendency toward self-blame could also have originated in the family of origin with an angry father or mother. The child had no conception of what angered the parents, and internalized this rage as being unloved. This reenactment years later by the adult has its roots in the belief of not being loved, and the result is to look for love somewhere else.

Family Influences

Family influences can be a tough hurdle to live with. In most cases, families can enhance the marriage by bringing support, warmth and continuity. But in some cases, family influences can divert you from the primary goals of marriage and take you onto the tortuous path to divorce. Such influences often take the form of loyalties to parents or siblings while your spouse's welfare is put last on your list or cut out altogether. When that occurs, conflict is set in motion, unraveling the marriage goals.

The important thing to keep in mind is your hierarchy of loved ones. In that hierarchy your spouse comes first, then your children, your parents, your siblings and so on. The reason for that hierarchy is to protect your marriage from influences that can chip away at it.

For example, if your parents had a strong influence on you as a child, whether positive or negative, that influence will continue into your married life. Let's say that your mother or your father had a close relationship with you as you were growing up. You went fishing frequently with your father or you often drove your mother to errands, shopping or medical appointments. These pleasurable and charitable activities will be expected of you even when you are grown, married and working full-time.

Many parents will curtail these expectations out of consideration for the new responsibilities that a married man or woman will have. Other parents, however, object to the lack of attention and resent the spouse for "interfering" with their life. Their resentment may be unconscious, but consciously they will make a critical survey of the spouse's behavior and complain about lack of attention or anything else they might object to. Their objection is to simply feeling unloved, on the unconscious level. That is when you need to become resourceful and find ways to accommodate them and let them know you still love them. You need to make them understand that you are now fully occupied in your married life and that you have to curtail some of the activities you shared with them in the past. Look for ways to compensate your parents for not sharing these activities any longer. Find special occasions to treat them kindly such as sending flowers unexpectedly, treating them to a complimentary sauna or massage, or a dinner for the three of you at their favorite restaurant. When these little attentions come their way, they will feel loved and know they are still special to you.

Illness

Illness can also bring woes if the partners have unfinished business. In most cases, illness brings on newfound love and affection for the ill partner. In other cases, an illness can become the reason one partner seeks to exit the marriage. Serious illnesses, incurable diseases such as cancer, or infectious diseases such as AIDS can become the ax that will test or shatter the marriage. (Here is a good place to be reminded that AIDS can also be contracted through infidelity, one-night stands and extramarital affairs, not only through a homosexual relationship or contaminated needles.)

This is also a good place to remind ourselves that "in sickness and in health" is part of this partnership in marriage. It is equally true that when your partner is ill, whether temporarily or with a serious illness, the stake in marriage is having someone to care for you when you are ill. To shrug off this part of your responsibility in the marriage is to invite problems later in life when you may be the one who needs loving care and attention.

When Contemplating the Final Step: Divorce

Marriage counseling to prevent divorce should be the next stage if everything else has failed. Working toward a solution to resolve conflict, whether through your own initiatives or through counseling, is the best remedy rather than remaining in a permanent paralysis. Again, you must remember that the grass is not always greener on the other side, your personal conflicts will not go away by being single or remarried, and your financial status will decrease as a result of the divorce. Divorce can contribute to a permanent financial deficit that becomes compounded by alimony and child support. In marriage, two heads are better than one and two people working together toward a common goal will find love and bliss.

When doubts or thoughts arise in your mind that you have had enough of this marriage, use the previous suggestions and the common goals of marriage (see the accompanying list) to prevent you from reaching for the divorce papers. Divorce is usually the easiest way out of responsibility, whereas working through a conflictful marriage takes patience. Your concentrated efforts to save the marriage will be rewarded in the end, giving you the pride of having preserved your married life together. This pride was once expressed memorably by a husband when he gratefully turned to his wife and acknowledged how she had been indispensable in helping him through trying times. Therapy and seeking help are extremely useful, but if the partners do not want to help themselves, no amount of therapy will help.

The Common Goals of Marriage

1. To cooperate with each other's personal goals in life.

2. To grow in an atmosphere of acceptance, love and faith in each other.

3. To elevate your family economic standards.

4. To raise a family with goals toward education.

5. To become the patriarch and matriarch who benefitted your future generations.

Exercise 8: My Goals in This Marriage

Turn now to your journal and list all the common goals you have for yourself and your spouse. You can use "The Common Goals of Marriage" as a base and add your own goals. Be as extravagant as you wish. Later you can scale them down to what is realistic now and what is possible in the future. Set a timetable for your goals. For example: your financial status in one year, five years, ten years and so on. Also list travel and pleasurable activities for you and your spouse and how you are going to make them happen.

Next, transfer this list to an index card (you can use the back side or two cards if your list is long) and always carry this card with you. In times of stress, strife or having lost your way, reread these goals. They are the innermost wishes your soul has revealed to you. Title this card "My Goals in This Marriage."

Conclusion

If you find yourself thinking that you have had enough of this marriage, *stop* and *look inward*. You know that a breakdown in communication, unfulfilled needs, physical or emotional abuse, a love-and-hate relationship, family reenactments, family influences, and illness will work against your marriage and can lead to divorce. Your *mission* is to stop and *clear the road* and continue on the path to *marital bliss*. Shed the fortress walls and leave yourself open to *love, affection* and *warmth*. Do not "pass the buck" out of anger and frustration from an unrelated source to your spouse. Direct these emotions to the proper source by resolving these conflicts at the appropriate time. Disclosing your frustrations to your spouse can be to your benefit. Remember that the *children* suffer terribly in a divorce. They become confused in their loyalties to their parents and their life is affected thereafter. Use a *red light* system when discussions get out of control. Above all, remember that your *spouse* will *work* with you if you let them know how much they are *loved* and how much *you want them*. That spouse will go to great lengths to help you in resolving your frustrations. Use the *common goals of marriage* to keep you in the *path of love*.

6

Our Defense Mechanisms

O, what a tangled web we weave,
when first we practice to deceive!

—Sir Walter Scott

An unfulfilled adulthood has its roots in an unfulfilled childhood. If the child was abused, subjugated, or plain ignored, his instinctive survival mechanisms would surface to ward off danger and help meet his needs. But in most cases the results may have been faulty at best. An unfulfilled childhood will then carry over into adulthood, with all the accumulated unfulfilled desires ready to plague us daily. These unmet needs become repressed and unconscious. When they resurface now and then, our unconscious defense mechanisms are triggered to deal with them.

To help us understand how defense mechanisms work on our mind and behavior to repress our unacceptable impulses and desires, let us take a brief look at Sigmund Freud's theory of defense mechanisms. In 1923, Freud presented his theory of the three-part structure of the mind: the Id, the Ego and the Superego. In this model of the mind:

- The Id is the unconscious part made up of drives.
- The Ego is partly conscious and has the ability to reason.
- The Superego is also partly conscious and includes the conscience and unconscious feelings of guilt.

Early on, Freud also claimed that anxiety will cause repression, the basis for all defense mechanisms, when the Ego cannot deal with an internal danger to the psyche. With the help of his daughter, Anna Freud, Sigmund then postulated the Ego's defense mechanisms (Anna Freud, 1937, 1966). Defense mechanisms are triggered when: "The psyche is overtaken by the affect of anxiety if it feels that it is incapable of dealing by an appropriate reaction with a task (a danger) approaching from outside" (Sigmund Freud, 1926). In other words, if an individual feels threatened that he or she may lose the object of their affection or that their psyche may be subjected to an indescribable loss of safety, anxiety will emerge. Anxiety is therefore a signal from the Ego when there is a threat that a traumatic experience is about to occur. A threat or danger signifies a loss or separation of a love object that leads eventually to a feeling of helplessness. This helplessness results from "an accumulation of instinctual needs which cannot obtain satisfaction" (Freud, 1926).

In Freudian thought, the inability to obtain satisfaction is related to lack of skills or knowledge to resolve conflicts or problems that arise in any human relationships, and especially in married relationships. The Ego will then use its defense mechanisms to repress, operate, contain and control excessive anxiety or the fear of danger: the loss of love or a loved one. On the next page you will find a list of defense mechanisms.

Anna Freud's Ego Defense Mechanisms

Defense Mechanism	Definition and Characteristics
1. Repression	We *involuntarily* "push down" or repress unacceptable impulses into the unconscious.
2. Suppression	We *intentionally* prevent unacceptable thoughts from entering our consciousness.
3. Denial	We deny the knowledge that something is occurring that can threaten us with a loss, so we push it back into the unconscious temporarily or permanently, and are no longer threatened. Repression can occur when there is *denial that* a danger exists.
4. Projection	Sometimes we attribute our unacceptable impulses to another person. For example, if I don't like a certain trait about myself, I might *project* it onto someone else (attribute it to that person) and claim that I don't like this person because of that specific trait.
5. Displacement	At other times, after we repress a certain feeling toward someone we let it resurface by *displacing it* onto someone else. An example of displacement is being angry at one person but yelling at another person instead.
6. Sublimation	*Sublimation* occurs when we convert unacceptable impulses into a socially acceptable or creative activity that can repress our anxiety and help us avoid dealing with its reality.

Defense Mechanism	Definition and Characteristics
7. **Rationalization**	We *rationalize* when we try to justify our wrongdoing. For example, we convince ourselves that because something is due to us we can either cheat or appropriate it.
8. **Regression**	Sometimes we *regress* when we feel it is more safe and comfortable to remain in a primitive or earlier developmental stage.
9. **Reaction formation**	At other times, we deal with anxiety by doing the opposite of what we feel. For example we may repress our dislike or fear of someone and instead become nice to them. An extreme example of *reaction formation* is when war prisoners become totally accepting of their jailers' ideology to repress their fear of torture or death.
10. **Intellectualization**	This defense mechanism takes place when we use excessive intellectual terminology to avoid having to feel something that is too difficult to experience.
11. **Fantasy**	We can gratify ourselves through *fantasy* of activities and feats when our desires are frustrated.
12. **Compensation**	We can also *compensate* for a lack in one area by overgratifying or overachieving in another area.
13. **Identification**	At times we can *identify* with an aggressor whose traits we fear or we can *identify* with famous personalities to give us a sense of worth.
14. **Introjection**	We can also *introject* another's admired characteristics and make them our own.

Defense Mechanism	Definition and Characteristics
15. Emotional insulation	We can avoid being hurt by withdrawing into *emotional insulation*.
16. Isolation	We *isolate* unacceptable thoughts in consciousness to separate them from emotions or connecting ideas. Also a form of *compartmentalizing* acceptable from unacceptable thoughts and is characteristic of obsessive-compulsive behavior. (Fenichel, 1945).
17. Undoing	The last defense mechanism, *undoing*, mean to counteract or atone for an unacceptable thought or act and is a characteristic in an obsessive-compulsive personality.

Reprinted by permission from Monte, 1991; Anna Freud, 1937, 1966; Undoing and Isolation examples from Fenichel, 1945; Sandler & A. Freud, 1985.

These defense mechanisms are set in motion when the Ego does not want to deal with unacceptable impulses, so it represses them in the unconscious. Repression in an individual, for example, is a symptom that the ego has repressed the fear that a danger exists, thereby making the individual helpless to stop it. We can gain insight about ourselves and others by keeping these defense mechanisms in mind.

Every one of us has some fear such as losing love or something of value to our survival. This imminent fear is so great that we repress it instead of facing and resolving it. We need to be aware of our human emotions and defense mechanisms to help solve and eliminate conflicts, and alleviate debilitating anxiety and vague apprehensions about danger to our integrity. We can begin by learning to verbalize this danger and put it in proper perspective. If, for example, our spouse is unresponsive, we may immediately attribute their lack of attention to a lack of love for us. This fear of not being loved can cause us to become moody and anxious. As we learn the reasons for our partner's and our own moods and behavior, we can learn to rectify erroneous thoughts and resolve conflicts. Similarly, symptoms such as bodily illnesses caused by unresolved conflicts can be remedied.

Repression, one of the basic defense mechanisms, tells our consciousness that everything is okay. It serves to cover and bury an unacceptable thought or action we do not want to face or resolve. Resolving an issue or problem usually involves having to admit that all is not well with us. In addition, it takes work and patience to resolve an unpleasant issue or problem. When we repress, deny or bury a problem, it does not go away. It festers while being buried. Compare, if you will, a compost pile to buried problems. Compost is an accumulation of grass clippings, leaves and vegetable waste that becomes fertilizer for gardens. While a pile of compost lies in a heap it generates heat that decomposes organic matter. The gardener then turns the pile over and over to let the heat escape while decomposition takes place. When we bury a problem we constantly use mental energy to keep the memory from resurfacing. It takes less energy to resolve a problem than to keep it repressed for days, months or years.

A problem that is not resolved will affect another new issue and add to it. As you pile up problems one on top of another, more energy is used up leaving you drained, deeply depressed, or exploding at inappropriate times.

෧ ෧ ෧

A Case Study

For example, Jean suspects that her husband John is having an affair. Her suspicion is based on the fact that he ignores her, leaves early in the morning, often comes home late at night, and is almost never hungry when he gets home. Jean is wracked with anxieties and cannot bring herself to confront John. She then occupies her time by being extremely busy so as not to think about John's absences from her life. Jean's life is overwhelmed with busyness but her energy is low. She feels tired most of the time and suffers from recurring colds and flu.

∽ ∽ ∽

If we look at Jean's family history, we will see a pattern of neglect from her father and mother. Jean felt unloved while growing up and had no voice to air her complaints. To Jean, pain was a daily occurrence that turned her into a shy and withdrawn child. She learned, gradually, not to feel the pain by denying it. Subconsciously, Jean used a repressive mechanism to deny that her relationship with John is faltering or, worst, non-existent.

We deny problems not only because we do not know how to deal with them, but also because they have a way of bringing up pain. This pain may not be associated with a present event. Pain has a way of lodging into our subconscious brain memory, then rears its head when triggered by a past or present association. When pain is not resolved or understood it becomes an abscess. In Jean's case, John's complete disregard for her needs may have triggered the same pain of being unloved as a child and being ignored by her parents. The mechanisms of repression and denial in Jean's life have been in place and operating since childhood. If Jean had understood that the problem with John was not so much her fault but her inability to deal with pain, she would have opened up and spoken to him about it.

Our defense mechanisms against danger may have possibly existed in a collective unconscious blueprint since ancient history. In the cave days of prehistoric times, for example, survival of the fittest involved stealing meat from another to feed ourselves. Our ancestors may have submitted themselves to subjugation in exchange for protection by the cave leader against predators. Think of a collective unconscious as a genetic blueprint that is handed down to you through your historical ancestors. We still have no scientific data to account for various genetic traits manifested in behavior and passed down through our ancestors' line. There is, however, a body of evidence to suggest that not only eye color, hair color, and height are handed down to offspring through genetics but also characteristics such as a talent for dancing or painting or math and science ability (Steele, Lindley, & Blanden, 1998).

Other defense mechanisms such as *projection* and *displacement* serve the purpose of getting rid of unacceptable impulses, thoughts or feelings and dumping them onto someone else. For example, if John had feelings of sexual inadequacy and therefore a need for outside validation by other women, he may have chastised a friend at work for exhibiting the same behavior, an example of *projection*. When John did come home early, sometimes he would yell at Jean for not having his dinner ready, *displacing* his anger at her. That outburst gave him the *rationalization* and justification to continue his destructive behavior. John had also come from a background where his father was unfaithful to his mother, then yelled at the whole family when his needs were not satisfied.

Jean, on the other hand, *sublimated* her anxiety and loneliness by becoming extremely occupied with charity events, art classes, and volunteer work on behalf of several organizations. Those activities took precedence over her household responsibilities and taking care of their three children. Jean also displayed *reaction formation* behavior whenever John came home late. Instead of showing her hurt and anger, she would make it a point to prepare a late-night snack for him in case he was hungry. Her fear of losing John even though he totally ignored her kept her from expressing her anger, just as she had been afraid of expressing anger at her parents for fear of losing them. In addition, Jean was split down the middle about her relationship with John. She confided to her close friend, Sarah, that she stopped having sex with her husband because she had no love for him, yet she became seductive and playful the minute he came home. Jean had *compartmentalized* her emotions because of the conflicting feelings she had toward John.

Meanwhile John would sexually *fantasize* about nearly every woman he saw or encountered at work and elsewhere. John's libido was operating on overdrive by the age of forty. He had fallen into a sexual addiction he could neither control nor understand, and it was undermining his relationship with Jean and his children. After a period of sexual overactivity he would subconsciously atone (*undoing*) by attending church every Sunday, but then stop and fantasize again and the cycle would repeat itself.

Jean and John's case exemplifies childhood dysfunctions carried as emotional baggage into adulthood. The defense mechanisms operating in their psyches were survival methods they used to avoid dealing with reality. Through early role-modeling in John's home and repressing pain in Jean's case, they adapted and created their own rules for daily life. It was only when they hit bottom—when John discovered that he had given Jean venereal disease—and Jean could no longer deny the truth staring her in the face that they mutually agreed to seek help. Many times in life we close our minds and eyes to unpleasant truths that can hurt us emotionally. In time we hurt ourselves more deeply and inflict lifelong scars upon ourselves and loved ones.

Conclusion

Our *defense mechanisms* repress unacceptable impulses and excessive anxiety over the fear of losing a love object. Anxiety signals the Ego that a threat or traumatic experience is about to occur. Be aware of your defense mechanisms, especially *repression* as the basis for all the mechanisms.

Excessive fear of losing love or something of value for our survival can make us feel helpless. Therefore, we repress our fear. Once we become aware of our defense mechanisms, we can better understand and control our behavior instead of those mechanisms controlling us.

7

The Unique
Individual: You

The mold is broken as soon as we are born

Throughout this book I would like you to keep in mind that you are a unique individual, that no one can take away your individuality and right to foster your dreams. As we discussed in the preface of this book, two unique individuals unite in marriage to bring their essence to this institution. That essence, illuminated with love, flourishes and sparkles like a diamond that reflects the joys of two lives being fulfilled. Often, to be an individual is to go against the grain of what we have been taught. We want to leave our mark in the world by being unique and different from any other being. Therefore, we feel compelled to do things differently and sometimes contrary to common sense. This is how we proclaim we are not sheep and that we will not follow the herd. The hippie revolution of the sixties proclaimed that we were going to question our elders and government authority. The Vietnam War too began an era of conscious soul-searching.

Sometimes, however, to be a unique individual is to exert our mind power and bend with the rules. You might say at this point, this is contradictory. That is quite true, but only on the surface. By taking a flexible approach we can observe, learn and study what we would like to change for

the best. That is, in a marriage fraught with conflicts, we
need to use our individuality and learn what we can do or
contribute to this marriage so that our uniqueness and
individuality may thrive. Two people who make a
commitment that their marriage is worth saving will use
their individuality and unique power of mind to save their
marriage.

❧   ❧   ❧

A Case Study

When two individuals clash in a marriage that is
choked by repression and power over one another, it is
time to examine where it went wrong and what
contributed to its demise. In the case of a couple we shall
call Jim and Stacey, their arguments always centered on
family ties. "Jim can't stand my family and constantly
criticizes both my brother and my father," said Stacey.
Jim's complaint is that Stacey won't concede to his
mother's wishes that Stacey call her at least once a week.

❧   ❧   ❧

Both Jim and Stacey are using their power to assert their
individuality that they are right. Meanwhile they are using
their life energies in a negative way. Every time they clash
and become fixed in their opinion, a small stone is chipped
away from the marriage building. Instead, they could try to
meet half way and compromise. If Jim works on
withholding his criticism of Stacey's family as long as he
can, and on finding out what it is he does not like about
them, he then can add another stone to the marriage. In that
process he can identify the cause of his dislike by asking
himself: "Why does it bother me that Stacey's brother is
pushy or overpowering?" "Why does her father ignore my
success in business?" By probing within, he may come up

with answers such as: "Perhaps her brother's pushiness reminds me of a time in high school when this guy took away..., " "Her brother's overpowering manners may be a cover up for his own deep feelings of insecurity," "Her father may be feeling sadness at not having done the same in his younger years."

In each instance, rather than reacting with criticism Jim should ask himself questions. In the end all these minor irritations have nothing to do with him, nor with Stacey for that matter. Jim should weigh the consequences: If these conflicts are outside the marriage, why should he own them and inflict them upon his marriage? By examining, probing and asking questions, Jim can take it upon himself to be an individual and decide whether to absorb the conflicts or let them flow out the marriage door.

Stacey, on the other hand, will probe Jim's insistence on calling his mother and ask herself, "Why does she want me to call her every week? Is she lonely?" Rather than feeling burdened by being expected to call, Stacey can look into the reasons for her mother-in-law's request. Is it because she can't force her son to call her and knows that her daughter-in-law is sympathetic to another woman's plight? By merging with her mother-in-law's viewpoint, Stacey will gain an understanding of a woman living alone, and with Jim's appreciation of her understanding, she will feel their mutual love grow.

The reasons for a man's or woman's motivations can be numerous. By probing into the behavior, the reluctance or aloofness of your partner, you can begin to understand their motivations.

Understanding My Spouse's and My Own Behavior

My Spouse's Behavior	My Behavior/Reaction
Hypersensitive to criticism.	I don't understand why he/she can't take my advice.
Not looking when I'm speaking.	I get ticked off when he/she looks away when I'm talking.
Self-centered, non-stop talk.	I feel left out.

Following such an examination of your partner's motivations, you can gently remind them that your advice was well-intentioned and non-critical. You can point out that you like to make eye contact when you are talking to them, and you can interrupt their continuous talking by smiling (if you can) and saying in a firm voice, "I'd like to say something now."

Exercise 9: The Reasons Behind People's Behavior

At this point, turn to your journal and write down instances in your life where you ran head-on into someone's objection, criticism or plain rejection. Take a good look at that event and what the result was. Be honest with yourself and probe the reasons for the conflict. There is no need to be afraid of the truth; no one is there but yourself, so no one will laugh at you or criticize the answer. Try to uncover the other person's motive for acting that way. Nine times out of ten you will discover it was something in their past that made them behave in a certain way toward you. And sometimes, if you are completely honest, you will realize that you behaved in a certain manner toward them that made them critical or rejecting of you. Now take an index card and title it "The Reasons Behind People's Behavior," and list some examples including your own behavior.

When we react strongly to others' behavior, we need to stop and ask ourselves why these behaviors bother us so much. Is it because when we were little no one listened to us and now when we make a point we are too forceful? Or perhaps the other person was raised in a highly critical home where their voice was silenced?

Every one of our past behaviors, choices and decisions had to do with the way we were brought up and what motivated us. But now in the present and in the future we can untangle ourselves from all the deadweight that motivated our actions. We can then choose the path to rediscover our unique self. This is the path that each one of us will create in our own unique way. In the end, when you finally discover the unique person that has emerged, you will know who you really are, and that no one can mold you into their own image. This, therefore, is the true essence of what you have been born to achieve. By looking into the motivations for another person's action, you have merged with them and in the process have found yourself.

If we think about the generational dysfunctions caused by physically and emotionally absent fathers and by distant mothers who lacked their husband's love and support, as well as the emotional baggage they both brought into the marriage, we can see why offspring carry their ancestors' scars.

Exercise 10: Genealogical Characteristics

Now is a good time to use as sample the genealogical chart at the end of the book and fill in your family tree, not only the names of relatives but also their characteristics as far back as you can remember. Again, this is an exercise for your eyes only. No one else has to see your interpretation of your parents, siblings and other relatives.

In the genealogical chart, jot down every characteristic you noticed in your father, mother, aunts, uncles and grandparents as you were growing up that either excited, scared, mystified or left you untouched. Write down any dreams or regrets they communicated to you. If, for example, your father was supportive and was there for you most of the time, then this is what you will record. If, on the other hand, he was absent, too busy, critical or violent, then this should also be noted. How was your mother affected by her relationship with your father? Did she complain or just remain silent? Now go one generation up to both sets of grandparents. What were their characteristics? What did they expect from your parents as they were growing up? Now skip down to your children and record your expectations of them. If you do not have children, jot down what you would want your future offspring to be or accomplish for themselves.

In the Similar Traits or Behavior chart, in the spaces provided, write in each line the connections or similar characteristics you discovered between you and your father and mother. Do the same for characteristics between you and your grandfathers and grandmothers. Did you inherit an artistic temperament from your mother? Have you found yourself repeating the same instructions or criticisms to your spouse or children? Remember that every event, be it joyful, frightening or lonely, that was recorded by your brain became permanent in your psyche. Just like the saying "History repeats itself," we unconsciously repeat experiences or hurts and pass them on to a new generation. Somehow, not only do we pass our genes to our offspring but also our behavioral tendencies with all their consequences.

Your Uniqueness

Everyone has characteristics in common with their ancestors, but also unique, individual traits. These unique traits were "blueprinted" within you as you grew up and observed the world around you. Envision for a moment a cook making a pot of soup. One time the cook will add a little more salt and less pepper to that soup. The next time might be the opposite, the soup less salty but spicier. In a similar way, somehow the pool of genes varies slightly to create the unique concoction that is you. Think of the millions of fingerprints in police records, agencies and work institutions such as banking where employees have to be bonded: no two individual fingerprints are alike.

Even though, for example, you wanted to emulate your father's skills or your mother's endeavors, you decided to choose in childhood what you wanted most in your adult life. In any case those wishes were slightly or totally different than your parents' established skills. But "Ay, there's the rub," as Hamlet said. Even as your strongest wishes revealed themselves and led you to pursue a different path from your ancestral one, your psyche told you to stay the course and follow the same path your parents set for themselves. That is where conflict will arise and set you at a dead end or split you to the point of not wanting anything to do with your father or mother. Their presence, after all, is always with you urging you to do the same as they have or have not done.

In many families well-meaning parents want the best for their children. They will stand behind them in their quest for independence and support them along the way. However, in some cases, the parents may want the best for their heir but are ambivalent about it. If, for example, the father aspired during his youth to be an engineer but failed to become one, he may have internalized the thought that since he did not succeed therefore his son or daughter cannot succeed either. The subconscious wish for failure is so strong that in no way can his successor be successful. After all, shouldn't every child grow up to be like his dad or mom? Children grow up taking their cues from parents and model themselves upon the only example set before their eyes.

The most important fact to remember is that you are unique, that you own your own thoughts and feelings and no one can negate them. Since those unique feelings emerged from within you, they are yours and you retain exclusive rights over them. Although you may have inherited biological traits from your parents, you are a separate entity in thoughts, feelings and goals in life.

Exercise Progress

By now, hopefully, you have mastered Exercises 1 through 10 and are on your way to thinking clearly about your marriage goals and the outside influences on this marriage. Spend five to ten minutes each morning reviewing your index cards. If you have not done so, please go back and practice and review these exercises. The difference between changing patterns not beneficial to your welfare and progressing in your life is dedicating yourself to that important cause.

Conclusion

You are *unique*. To be unique is to exert your mind power to bend with the rules and to observe, study, and analyze your environment to change things for the best. We assert our individuality in *resolving conflicts* by probing, examining and asking questions rather than by reacting in kind to criticism. These conflicts will then flow out the marriage door. We again *merge* with the conflicting individual and examine their requests, resistance or aloofness. Aloofness, rejections or criticisms are needs in disguise. Satisfied needs bring harmony and love into the marriage. Know your genealogy and how characteristics and behaviors were passed down to you from generation to generation. *You own your own thoughts and feelings that no one can negate.*

— 8 —

How to Love Yourself

---

*It is a funny thing about life; if you refuse to
accept anything but the best, you very often get it.*

—Somerset Maugham

Have you ever asked yourself what you can do to please
your spouse or partner? Of course you have, at
holidays, birthdays, anniversaries and special days. We all
want to please loved ones and sometimes we bend over
backwards to do so. Have you ever asked yourself, though,
how can I please myself or do I love myself? That is a
difficult question to ask of oneself. We only tend to see our
worth mirrored in others' actions and behavior toward us. It
is the measure by which we constantly gauge our worth, our
lovableness and place in the world. Is this then how we want
to spend the rest of our lives, waiting for someone to love
us? It would be tantamount to being a puppy wagging its
tail and waiting for that hand to caress it. Sure we all want to
be loved, but love has to start within us.

How then are we to tackle this age-old dilemma? On one
hand we want love and on the other we do not feel worthy of
being loved. If we did love ourselves, then we would have
no doubts about being loved. Or if I love myself, how can it
be that no one loves me? Having these doubts about being
loved is enough to want to retreat within oneself.

Do You Love Yourself?

How can we know if we love ourselves? To begin with, we look at how we treat ourselves overall. The way we can test this question is how we care for ourselves on a daily basis, how we take care of our appearance, our health and our welfare. If I love myself then I will be dressed according to my worth. I will make sure my body is not starved and I will exercise good judgment about my diet and physical health. These practices can be beneficial to an overall feeling of well-being and elevate our spirits.

Yet when it comes to love we are not sure. Will he like my looks? Will she find me witty and handsome? Do we look for a mate to spend the rest of our lives with, or do we look for someone to validate who we are? Again that is a difficult question. We decide after courtship that "this is the person I have been looking for all my life; she or he is what I dreamt of, and I must bond with them now that I found that irreplaceable person." The only thing wrong with this line of thinking is that there could be a hundred reasons for falling in love with that particular person.

Let's start with the reason that he or she looks like the ideal you forged a long time ago. That may have started in childhood with the caregiver who supplied the mold upon which you based yourself. We begin to forge an image of our ideal mate by imprinting what our eyes fell upon at our first gaze into this world. With repeated sightings we became familiar with and learned to love the image we saw from our crib. That first image was most likely the mother, then the father. These two images are the blueprint upon which we model the kind of person we will marry in the end. Later in life when we meet total strangers, our brain will scan all the faces and behavior of those strangers.

If a man's mother, let's say, fit the image we shall call "ideal image" his brain will scan every female that fits that ideal image. If that lucky female has a similar look, certain gestures, behavior or even a particular way she brushed or held his hand, then she is "the one." For a woman the same rule applies. Her father's behavior, his expectations for her and even the way he loved her all compose the ideal blueprint of the man she will internalize in her subconscious. An abusive, unresponsive or unaffectionate parent will also be the mold that a man or woman will select as their "ideal" mate. Because our brain automatically scans that image for a *perfect fit*, a similar person will fit the mold in our subconscious.

◈   ◈   ◈

A Case Study

A good example is a couple I shall call Robert and Marie. Robert came from a divorced family, and Marie from a family where her parents were still married. Robert grew up without a father and lacked a sense of identity. Since his mother was the only one he could identify with, he compensated for his lack of a father through other pursuits such as traveling, adventure and a thirst for women. He pursued women before and after he met Marie to reassure and prove to himself that he was a desirable man, since he had not experienced the role model of a male image in the home. Robert nevertheless had received a fair amount of love from his mother, but she could not replace the father he craved. Only his father's love could affirm that he was worthy of being loved. In Robert's case a lack of love for himself molded him throughout his life: he lacked the proper education to advance himself, flirted with dead-end relationships and manifested self-destructive behavior.

Although Marie had come from a two-parent home, she had not received love or affection from either parent and was a physically battered child. When she met Robert she became enchanted by his looks, charm and ability to seduce her. She then interpreted all the attention he showered on her as love, an emotion she had experienced very little while growing up. However, the trigger for marrying Robert came one day when he became very angry at her for accidentally spilling a cup of coffee on him. After the initial shock she forgave the incident. She did not know then that her brain had scanned similar incidents from the past when her father, who was an angry man, would become enraged at her over petty offenses. Her subconscious mind had internalized this model as her image of a man. It was Marie's subconscious submissiveness to abuse that won Robert's heart, the same way his mother endured his father's infidelities and power control.

Robert and Marie shared other traits and pursuits in common. They both loved adventure and travel and the rugged outdoors. This gave them a sense of freedom they lacked while growing up. Their childhoods had given them a sense of narrowness and claustrophobia: fear of being poor for Robert and no room to develop a self-identity for Marie.

Later in life, after years of marital dysfunction and unhappiness, Robert and Marie came to understand that their self-destructive life together was patterned upon their upbringing, and only then did they rediscover the real love they had for each other. The love they had searched for all their lives was always there, hidden by the emotional baggage they had brought into the marriage. They could not love each other during those trying years because they did not love themselves—much the same way that their parents could not impart this love to them due to their own dysfunctions. These trying years were replayed as a reenactment of their parents' destructive life, until the couple hit bottom. They both understood then that the type of love they craved would always elude them. It was only the real love they had for each other that was alive and longing to be released.

☙   ☙   ☙

Learning to Love Yourself

How can we begin to examine our lives and break free of the dysfunctions and the love starvation diet we have imposed upon ourselves? We can start by seeing ourselves and our spouse as human beings with faults and frailties but nonetheless with the power of love within. This love is within everyone whether we have experienced it or not. The ones who were lucky enough to have experienced it fully will apply themselves to it. The ones who were starved of this wonderful human emotion called love will still have the capacity for it. This built-in love potential is what will motivate everyone to search for it all their lives.

How then can we retrain and condition ourselves to tap this love source within us? We can begin by telling ourselves that we are strong in our unbounded capacity to love. We can also look for good things we did in the past. If it is hard for you to remember them, you now have the opportunity to start them anew. These can be anything from helping your spouse with the groceries, to helping an old person cross the street or other good deed that might come your way. Grab that opportunity to bring forth this love inside yourself.

Another way is to take some time off by yourself and reexamine your childhood. Look into your mind's eye and see yourself as a little child. You can use a childhood photo of yourself and try to visualize the lovable attributes that were and still are in you. Think about the innocence in your eyes in that photo and the wish to be noticed and hugged and kissed. On any day when you pass a child on the street and smile at their innocence and their lovable qualities, you are that child. You are looking inward at yourself as a child. You too are all those things because the child that is inside you always walks alongside you.

Another way to love yourself is to see yourself through someone else's eyes. Stand in front of a mirror and imagine for a moment that the image you see in the mirror is not you but someone else — preferably a person who values and likes you: for example, a special friend. Now imagine that you change places and you are that friend standing in front of the mirror looking at you in the mirror. What would your friend say about you now? Perhaps that you're a true friend, dependable, or a caring person. Now say these things out loud to the mirror and repeat them at least five to ten times. You can also bring out the features you like best about yourself, such as "I like the color of my eyes" or "I feel comfortable with my weight — I don't need to change a thing unless my health is at stake, and I don't have to torture myself with crash diets just to please someone else."

The way you look at someone else with love is the way I want you to look at yourself. Stand in front of the mirror and tell yourself: "I am a lovable person." "There are good things about me." "I want to love and treat myself kindly the way I would treat others." "Looking at myself with someone else's eyes, I know they would see me as a good person inside and ready to open myself to mirror back this love to them."

Imagine now for a few minutes that you can look inside your body. You zoom in with a camera and get close to your heart. See that heart beating and feeding blood to your arteries. That heart is beating autonomously with the sole function of feeding your cells, brain and other organs to keep you alive. Somehow, the organism that is you has the duty and obligation to keep you alive and well. Now zoom in even closer and see the cells in your body renewing themselves and sustaining your whole person. You can then feel the amazement of seeing a life, your life. It is a pure miracle to have life thriving in you. It is also your duty to sustain that amazing miracle that is you. Anything less is unacceptable. This life of yours from its inception, from the one cell that grew into the person you are now, is miraculous. Feel the entrustment placed in your hands to protect this life while you are viewing yourself as if through a microscope.

Now step back and distance yourself from that image and see yourself as a tiny being, so small that you can hold yourself in your two hands. If you were holding someone else other than you, could you have compassion for that tiny being? Would you protect it from any harm that might obliterate it? Of course you would. We all have this compassion inside us because we are human. Take a good look at that defenseless being, for it is you. You are here in this life to protect yourself from any harm that threatens from within and from without.

To protect the life that is in your custody you have to cherish and love yourself. You have to take care of your body and stop judgmental thoughts and criticism toward yourself. You have to be patient with yourself. You have to accept your shortcomings and faults. You have to stop torturing and terrorizing yourself with negative thoughts and be kind to yourself. In short, you are here for you.

Exercise 11: I Will Love Myself as Others Love Me

Turn to your journal and write down all the good things about yourself. Don't be shy—exaggeration is permissible. We are so hard on ourselves that we do not admit the good things we possess. So exaggerate and acknowledge those good things about yourself. Anything you write down is coming out of you. On an index card transfer those qualities that have been buried for years inside you and free them. This card is to be read each day if possible or several times per week. Keep this card with you or easily accessible. Title this card "I Will Love Myself as Others Love Me."

When you have mastered this card you will repeat these things to yourself in times of stress and when you are feeling down or negative about yourself. As soon as you feel your mood changing into negative feelings, bring out that good inventory you listed on that card. With practice you will be able to change a depressive feeling to one where things are not so bad after all, even if you are in a conflict or high-stress mode. By repeating the good inventory you will be able to focus on what is troubling you and resolve the conflict. A tremendous amount of energy is used up in feeling anger, rage, resentment or depression. Instead you can release this powerful energy to be creative, to love yourself and to love others. Loving yourself can not only give you a sense of peace and safety but also bring forth the love you want from your spouse. The way that we are attracted to a child's innocence and lovable appearance will be the same way that someone else will see you. They will see the love inside you flow to them and then back to you.

The Power to Be Free of Negativity

We all have the power to free ourselves from any situation. Imagine for a moment that your ship was about to sink. You would frantically run to the lifeboats available. Your next challenge would be to survive on an island. You would search for a food source from dawn to dusk until you find it — unless the coconuts were lying right there at your feet on the beach. Whenever we are in a life-threatening situation, our instinctive "survival manual" comes up from our brain's labyrinth. This survival manual has been pro-grammed and blueprinted from infancy when hunger pain first stirred us. It is built into all of us; it only needs to be dusted off and reactivated.

In times of stress, we need to be able to reach into this survival manual and put it to use immediately. The best way to make it active is to catch and observe yourself while you are in a downward-spiraling mood or just about to blow up. You are then to pause if you can. It will take immense concentration to take yourself out for a split second and be able to say out loud: "Stop! Stop! Stop! Stop!" Say the directive word "Stop!" as many times as you can. The effect is like an out-of-body experience, from an obsessive spin to an observation of yourself. You can also clap your hands together to emphasize the directive as you say the words "Stop! Stop! Stop!" Think of yourself as the director of a motion picture giving the film crew the directive "Stop!"

Exercise 12: Stop! Stop! Stop!

First read this exercise, then close the book and do it. Standing in front of a mirror, close your eyes and recollect an unpleasant memory, one that brings a painful association. As you think about that event, observe your feelings as if you were looking down at yourself. When you begin to feel a downward mood and pain flooding your senses, raise your head and say out loud to the mirror: "Stop! Stop! Stop!" Now move away from the mirror and repeat that exercise several times with the "Stop!" directive.

Every time you find yourself in a downward spiral due to unpleasant memories, exercise the "Stop!" directive until you have mastered it. With practice you will find that the painful recalls will flee away without any attempt on your part to stop them and your mood will remain stable. What happens in this case is a reprogramming in your psyche that this memory is acceptable and will no longer hurt you. That memory has no more power over you and you now have the power to be its master. Now do the exercise.

The Power to Feel Good

Whenever we are feeling bad emotionally or have negative thoughts, we tend to fall into an obsessive trance. Feeling bad drains our life energies and we tend not only to experience this mood but to indulge it. The more we feel bad the more we get used to that feeling until it becomes so familiar that we cannot live without it. We then feel comfortable in feeling bad! After a while this familiar bad feeling becomes so unbearable that we don't feel comfortable at all. A vicious pattern then sets in that contributes to obsessive thoughts and behavior, making us miserable. That is when we finally get the attention we have been craving. People around us will sympathize with our misery and say kind words to us. Instead of getting this sorry attention, what if we could get the opposite? Like "He has a great sense of humor," or "She makes me feel good because she's so upbeat; I like being around her."

When we have bad feelings it gives us a sense of power: the power to make ourselves miserable. We have the power to feel bad, but we also have the power to feel good. This power can be switched at will, once you become its master. We also have power over our own thoughts and the actions resulting from these thought patterns. In Chapter 3 we saw that the source of conflict can often originate from own thought patterns or irrational beliefs not the words or actions of someone else. If we acquire a pattern of irrational beliefs, we may follow a course of erroneous self-reasoning. In the same way that we can channel our reasoning into a dead-end alley of negative thoughts, we can also channel our thinking into a free—flowing avenue of positive thoughts. No one can take the power of positive thinking from us; it belongs to us and we are its master.

Exercise 13: I Am Powerful

On an index card put down these words in capital
letters: "I HAVE THE POWER TO FEEL GOOD AND
BE FREE!" You can use colored pens, or better yet, write
these words in gold ink signifying what they are worth.
This card should be duplicated and kept in your
pockets, at home, in your car or anywhere else to remind
you of who you really are: a free and a good person. Title
this card: "I Am Powerful."

Conclusion

Each one of us is a *unique* individual. Your *life* is a pure
miracle. The power of *love is within us*. We must love
ourselves because we have the *duty* and *obligation* to *survive*
and make this life *thrive* and *grow*. We have the *power* and we
are the *masters* over our *lives*. When we feel down or
spiraling into dark moods we use the "Stop! Stop! Stop!
Stop!" repetition to step out of that mood. Bad memories or
painful feelings cannot hurt us because they have no power
over us. We have the *power* over that memory. We also have
the *power to feel good and be free*.

— 9 —

Threats to the Marriage: His and Hers

We're not endowed with real life. And all that seems most real about us is but the thinnest substance of a dream until the heart be touched. That touch creates us.

—Nathaniel Hawthorne

From time immemorial man and woman met, fell in love and bonded in marriage. The words pronounced at the altar, "What God has united let no man break asunder," are a warning to the outside world. Those words are the essence of the marriage commitment. Nothing on earth should break this union unless love has died between a couple or when death do them part. Those words also warn us that when two people love each other no other being or outside influence should break this union. This, though, is exactly what happens in many marriages. Not only do external circumstances threaten the marriage but the participants themselves can as well.

Sometimes, well into the first years of marriage, the finality and binding quality of marriage may make either spouse feel trapped in a commitment with no love, and possibly with abuse or danger to one's being. Those unfortunate conditions may or may not have been caused by the marriage itself. Some problems may have been brought into the union as emotional baggage. For example, feeling unloved could be caused by any one of many reasons such as not having been loved as a child and carrying this heavy stone into the relationship, or feeling not worthy of being loved. This burden can therefore set the scene beforehand as part of a pattern or anticipated outcome. Abuse, on the other hand, can be complex in its setting. Either spouse can initiate the abuse, and the other can allow it to continue because of fear, the consequent humiliation and exposure to the outside world, or a pattern originating in childhood. The overwhelming fear of monetary instability can also force a wife to endure continued abuse.

A series of motions or events takes place as soon as the marriage vows are pronounced. First the partners view the marriage as a sacred commitment and apply themselves to upholding and protecting it. A tug-of-war for power then comes into play. What better way is there to guard this precious union than to take charge right away? "I am in charge of this important task." The only trouble is, both partners want to be in charge and that creates the tug-of-war. For every person in charge there must be a person who reports to them. The minute a mishap occurs, it's his or her fault. After all, "I am in charge!" Almost everyone likes to be in charge and no one likes to be subjugated. That is, however, what occurs in most marriages and what leads to their downfall. One partner can become despondent and resentful when he or she allows the other to make all the decisions regarding their well-being and set restrictions on their freedom. The resentful partner will nevertheless resign in time to their bondage, but a tally is added every year until it all comes back one day like a boomerang.

How can we avoid falling into a marriage power trap? The answer lies in the marriage itself. If this partnership were a business venture, plans would be drawn and contracts lawfully signed. The marriage, however, is not a business. It is a verbal agreement with commitments, sharing and sacrifices. Although there is a marriage contract signature, there is no written document for personal conduct. Too often the unwritten guidelines for personal conduct are trampled, forgotten or swept under the rug with the rationalization that whatever is covered cannot be seen or felt.

In addition to the couple's lack of vision and false security in each other's trust, outside elements close in and encircle the marriage. Visualize the partners, if you will, as a couple of fugitives in a wagon fleeing from the poison arrows of their attackers. The arrows pierce through the wagon, each arrow labeled: emotional baggage, family influence, children's demands, society's demands, keeping up with the Joneses, job pressures, economic stresses, female and male predators looking for a different nest, etc., etc. The list is long. Awareness of these threats and how to deal with them is the answer.

Real threats do exist and undermine a marriage from the start. The thing to remember is that these threats will never go away. It's like wishing that war and poverty would go away. The awareness of those threats and how to avoid them is what this chapter is all about. Let us examine these threats as they pertain to each partner, and find out how to cope with and prevent inside and outside interference.

Myths: His and Hers

Several myths—the Machismo or the Amazing Lover mystique; the Successful Businessman; the Model Homemaker (or as I call them "The Stepford Wives," from a novel by Ira

Levin where every wife is an automated housewife designed by the husband to ensure domestic tranquillity)—still exert powerful influences on our lives. These days we also hear the words "commitment to the marriage." What does the word "commitment" mean? Is it a list of wants? Is it a list of verbal or written agreements? I keep hearing this "commitment to the relationship" catchphrase in the news, in the movies and in conversations. What does it mean exactly? When a woman says, "I want you to be committed to our relationship," does it mean she wants him to be on time for dinner, not look at other women, bring home a paycheck, or not keep secrets from her? When we use the word "commitment" we never ask for details or talk about it. So how does each partner understand what commitment entails? We will examine these questions, as well as the internal and external threats to the marriage for each partner.

The Machismo or Amazing Lover myth is prevalent in male-dominant societies and in the film and media industries. Merriam-Webster's dictionary defines machismo as... "1) a strong sense of masculine pride: an exaggerated masculinity; 2) an exaggerated or exhilarating sense of power or strength" (By permission. From *Merriam-Webster's Collegiate® Dictionary, Tenth Edition* © 2000 by Merriam-Webster, Incorporated). My ears always perk up when I hear the words "exaggerated" and "power." What does it mean when a man feels an exaggerated sense of power and pride in being masculine? Is it a sudden illumination that being powerfully masculine will enable a man to conquer the world? Should a man feel an exaggerated sense of power in being himself? I always thought that power comes from positive things we do for ourselves and for others. Real power is the ability to change a stagnant life to one that is vibrant and flowing.

If the myth of Machismo means that a man can give love to a woman by bringing her to orgasm, making her believe that she is really wanted and loved, then this man and woman are both deluding themselves. To the man, the woman is his conquest, a tally or a thing collected. This man will not marry her, be a father to her children or stand by her in times of grief, stress or trauma. Just when the woman needs this man, he will move on to newer conquests. The macho man values only his pleasure and abhors having to solve problems. That is the essence of the macho man and that is why he is compelled to drift from woman to woman.

Let us examine the myth of macho men as quint-essential, amazing lovers. In defining a sexual lover we must look into what makes a good sexual lover or sexual partner. The word "lover" means exactly what it says: to *love* someone with your heart, mind, body and soul. Loving only with the body is merely a quick physical act that leads to orgasm without the uplifting glow that comes from making love to someone you are in love with. Achieving orgasm becomes the one and only goal for the macho man. This repetitious act without real love becomes an addictive drive in his quest for other women. But this drive is insatiable because what he's really chasing after is the real love he craves but, for some unexplainable reason in his psyche, is unable to find on his own.

The other myth that also exerts powerful influence in disrupting a man's married life is having to be the Successful Businessman, the money making tree or the amazing provider. These powerful images are fed to males from childhood: "If you're not rich, you're nobody." This idea that "money makes the man" is carried into the marriage. The man then feels an obligation and duty to constantly increase his wealth at the expense of his personal life. Married career women can also fall into a similar Successful Businesswoman trap.

But the belief that money will bring love is an old and false one. The other way around is more accurate. Being loved and loving back can put you at the top of the world, wanting to conquer all riches. The exhilarating feeling of having earned or won a substantial amount of money is a short-lived feeling. As you get used to the idea of riches, this high feeling becomes worn-out and you have to produce more and more money to experience the same high. Although having all the money in the world may buy temporary love, it cannot bring the peaceful immersion one has from being loved as you are. Real love is also being loved for your love of laughter, your love of others dear to you, your love of stabilizing and protecting your life and that of others, and having the extraordinary power to love others as they are.

For the woman, the Model Homemaker myth also feeds into the insatiable myth of the superwoman or supermother. None of these fictitious roles fits a real woman well. The only reward this myth brings is to enrich the creators of these roles found in popular women's magazines. These unrealistic expectations for women add more stress and induce a guilt trip on the woman already burdened with all the other roles she has to play. The young wife and mother finds herself all of a sudden overwhelmed and at the center of all those demands and expectations. She has to be the perfect wife, mother and housewife; a sexual woman, having to look good all the time; and an all-understanding being to her husband, children, parents, in-laws and others. In addition, if she works outside the home with the same stresses that her husband has in the work force, she still is burdened with the larger share of responsibility for the household. At the end of each day she has to look high and low for what is left of her and who she really is. When all her energies have been expended and extended to others, she is left like an empty shell. A real woman, in every sense of the word, is one who laughs with life, who lives intensely by savoring each moment and each day in her life, and who is appreciated by her family for her presence and contributions.

His World

For a man, the anticipation that marriage is the ground from which the fulfillment of all his desires will spring forth is the sure road to disappointment and disillusionment. The marriage and his wife will not satisfy financial and career goals. Remember that by the time a man marries he is supposed to have achieved at least some financial security. All right, so life is not always ideal and some men marry very young before they can advance financially. If that is the case, the hard realization that his marriage will not be a fountain of miracles should be fully understood and acknowledged. If his wife is willing to sacrifice her dreams and both partners are willing to forgo having children for a number of years, then it is possible for the wife to support her husband solely. This agreement may work for some couples. By the time a man has achieved his life dream, his wife is either exhausted from this arrangement or feels resentful to have put her goals in life on hold. It is twice as hard for the wife to defer her dreams and give her husband a sense of worth when she has not achieved her own dreams. The marriage therefore cannot give a man a personal sense of worth. He has to bring that legacy with him on the wedding day.

Another big stumbling block to a marriage is how the man views his wife overall. In the beginning it all seems so idyllic: she is beautiful, slim, sexual in every way and caters to all his needs. Then as the marriage progresses the picture changes: she is now pregnant and not as slim, and even though it is only for nine months, he feels short-changed. Now she is tired all the time from taking care of the children and the household and sometimes from working outside the home. She no longer looks appealing when he comes home. She may be disheveled, exhausted or in a lousy mood. That is when a man will start fantasizing and see that other women look better than his wife. Fantasizing, by the way, is pure one hundred percent wasted energy. Also, the line between fantasy and acting out can become blurred. That's when unfaithfulness slips into gear. That, of course, is the easy way out. Marriage commitment means constant work on ironing out the uneven edges.

Having an affair does not mean having a love affair. The adulterous affair is temporary. The participants lure themselves into believing that the other one is in love with them or cannot be without them. They have to hide and lie to have their trysts in hidden places or quickies in motels. While committing the adultery, other events fall into place. The first thing that happens to a man is distancing from his wife and children. He either is in a bad mood when he comes home, finds fault with everything, explodes at the slightest provocation or is miles away altogether. His job may suffer too; he becomes intolerant toward his co-workers, makes blunders or becomes plain dreamy. He may also withhold sex from his wife and may even suffer some impotence. After all, how much sex and lovemaking can he give her when he has already expended himself on the sidelines?

In the meantime his conscience will not sit idle. This built-in watchdog will cause him to slip and give it away through telltale signs such as lipstick smears, unfamiliar scents and hairs on his clothes, or receipts lying around. This conscience is his Superego, the internalization of his parents' punishment. That conscience caused him to punish himself by having the affair in the first place. An adulterous affair is a destructive force that gets set in motion when a man subconsciously feels that he needs to be punished — because in the end the punishment will be the divorce, if his wife finds out, and the upheaval that divorce brings.

When a man contemplates an adulterous affair, he needs to be aware and suspicious of the urge. He needs to ask himself, "Why do I want to jeopardize my marriage and destroy myself? What is it I need to be punished for?" He needs to consider, "Do I want to punish my wife? Is it because she put on weight? Is it because she doesn't have enough time for me? Shall I inflict traumatic pain on her because she has changed her appearance?"

On the wife's side, her husband's adulterous affair leaves her devastated with her entire world crumbling around her. The wounds and scars left in the wife are so deep that they never quite heal. At the slightest doubt, an alarm reactivates her anxieties, which then take over her entire life. The scars inflicted by a husband's adulterous affair are so debilitating that it takes years to heal and regain the shattered trust. For a woman the trauma of having been cheated on often presents a life-or-death question. A wife will feel this breach of trust as an attack on her entire being. She will feel trampled upon, diminished, reduced to zero, and her spirit and body violated. In some cases of unfaithfulness, women committed suicide while others became despondent with thoughts of suicide and long periods of depression. When they recovered, these women were never the same again. Their world had suddenly become a terrible and threatening place to be. The children also suffer in this trauma. They learn to take sides and have contempt for the father who committed the adultery.

Meanwhile, "the other woman" will not be happy just sitting on the side. She will want her commitment too: "divorce your wife or else." Another thing an adulterous affair cannot give a man is wholeness. It will not fill the voids inside him such as career or money goals. That other woman cannot fulfill those wishes. Instead, she will ask the man to fulfill her goals. That is why she went into the adulterous affair in the first place. In the end, two strangers searching for the same fleeting things will find only disappointment.

The adulterous man will never find the sense of fulfillment he is seeking. Lovemaking means exactly what it says: that sex without *love* is not fulfilling. Sex without love leaves a man unfulfilled and yearning for more insatiably without knowing what is missing. The other woman will not make him rich, handsome, taller or smarter. He will remain the same person afterwards, only in a much worse state.

Some final words of advice for the man: Rather than expending all that energy on adulterous affairs, it would be better focused on your wife. You could say, for example: "I love this little black dress on you," or "You have the most beautiful smile I ever saw," or "What can I do to help you?" A word of concern or encouragement will tap into her love for you, and she may find creative solutions to the alienation that existed between the two of you. By applying yourself creatively to removing the conflicts and obstacles in your way, you can have a clear path to love in your marriage. You can then go on to the blissful marriage that was always meant to be.

As you gradually increase the special time you spend together, as you express your thoughts and opinions to her and listen to hers, and when you make love to her, heaven will be there. She will return your love and be the sexual partner you always dreamt of in lovemaking. Remember always that in every woman there is the potential of being a love goddess. A woman is foremost a sexual being in her own right. She moves with her sexuality into paths of love. This is the path that you want to find and walk with her.

Exercise 14: How to Win Her Heart

This exercise is for the husband: In your journal describe in your own words what commitment means to you and how you would put it into action. Next write down a reasonable and realistic list of positive things you want to see in your wife. You can suggest ways for her to feel at ease if she is overwhelmed with her role as a wife or mother. Remember that if you want her to be more relaxed and have time for you, then you need to share in alleviating her load. You can take time off from your work and she from her family obligations to take mini vacations together. These can be a weekend trip, an afternoon drive to the ocean, a day in the country, or a secluded lunch in a small restaurant. These are priorities for enhancing your marriage. Next, transfer that list onto an index card and refer to it often. Title this card "How to Win Her Heart."

Her World

A woman's view of marriage differs from a man's. To a woman marriage is the safe harbor from storms, being with the man she enjoys making love with, and having him as the father of her children and the companion in her life's adventures. It also means being first in his life, even before his own mother. A woman will be mistaken, though, if she considers her husband as the man who will replace the ideal father or the father she never had. Sometimes the demands a woman makes on her husband are the very thing that alienates him. For example, she will either push him to careers that do not suit him or she may be indifferent. She can also browbeat him until he has no other alternative but to alienate himself from her. The demands that women put on their men are the same things they despised seeing in their mother's attitudes toward their own husband or father. A man should not be expected to perform amazing feats such as becoming fabulously rich, unless he initiates this wish. He should, though, provide a comfortable living for his family when his wife is physically unable to provide for herself and the children.

When thoughts of monetary dissatisfaction with your husband cross your mind, ask yourself: "Why am I so obsessed with wanting this new house, this trip or these clothes? Will these material possessions mean he loves me more? What if, instead, I get this love from him by being more seductive, holding him, or kissing his beautiful neck and ears every time I get a glimpse of them?" You will find, ten times out of ten, that the house, the trip or the clothes fade into the background when he reacts lovingly to your little kisses in strategic places.

The same expectation of faithfulness applies as much to women as to men. Another man will not replace your husband's qualities and willingness to spend the rest of his life with you. Another man will not fulfill you. Only you can do that by telling yourself that you are a unique individual with innate talents and a great capacity for love. So-called "love" given to a stranger will not bring any worthwhile returns. It will be wasted energy. The only thing that an adulterous affair will give you is the temporary illusion that you are admired and favored, while "the other man" enjoys his sexual conquest and gratification.

Another thing an adulterous affair will give you is a settling score with your parents if they themselves were divorced. This will be your punishment for them for all the ills they may have unconsciously imposed on you as a child or young adult. You may also unconsciously feel that if your parents were divorced, or married but unhappy, then it is also your lot in life: like parents, like children. But you are not your parents, and their lives are not yours. We would be no better off than chimpanzees, without a free will and unable to let our own individual creativity emerge from its bondage, if we were to copycat and model all the ills we saw. We are free to choose the best that life can offer us, and all you have to do is take it.

Men are just as vulnerable as women when it comes to their spouse's unfaithfulness. Although they may recover sooner from the shock and devastation, they still retain scars that will affect them over a lifetime. Not only will an adulterous affair cause him to lose trust in you, but any chance you had to win his heart might disappear altogether. The other dangers that also lurk with having sex outside the marriage are numerous: AIDS, herpes that may bring cancer of the uterus, gonorrhea and some strains of venereal diseases that do not respond to penicillin.

Some final words of advice for the woman: We women have a strange ability to push men's buttons, and tell them how to drive, where to park, how to conduct themselves and so on. This advice is well-intentioned but it drives a man crazy. In short, we are telling men that their performance is not acceptable and that it needs correction. Nothing is more annoying to a man than to be frequently corrected on past mistakes. This tendency to correct comes naturally from within us and from our natural instinct for nurturing. Our mothers, grandmothers, all the way up the genealogical tree, have done so before us. We, as well, are doing the same thing to our children, husbands and partners. The best technique a woman can use to her advantage to win her husband forever is to see him as a unique human being who may have faults but who is willing to win the world for her. This man of hers is to be pampered, loved, listened to with rapt attention, and made to feel that no other man can ever fill his shoes.

What a woman should avoid like the plague is to be a martyr, open to abuse and punishment. She should stand tall and sound her own voice. A woman should not feel that to be loved she must remain silent about her own views and opinions. She can express them gently without sounding pedantic, overpowering or deliberately contradictory. Also, asking for his advice can be an ego boost to the man who likes giving it.

Exercise 15: The Sound of My Own Voice

This exercise is for the wife: Turn now to your journal and list all your values, opinions and beliefs that are most important to you. For example, that women should be listened to and respected in their own right for their thoughts, voice and opinions without being made to feel foolish, or uninformed. Next take an index card and title it "The Sound of My Own Voice." Underneath this title you can list all those beliefs you have. This card should be kept accessible in your purse, on the car's dashboard, in your pocket or any other place where you will see it often.

The Aftermath of Infidelity

The trauma of having been cheated on is overwhelming for men, and even more so for women. For men it signifies a stripping of their malehood, a drilling at the core of their masculinity and integrity that leaves a deep hole in their psyche. Women, on the other hand, feel torn in two, their world crumbling and their trust in their partner obliterated altogether. With their safe world gone, the question that recurs over and over in their mind is where they've gone wrong — women have the tendency to blame themselves for having caused the alienation and infidelity by a lack of nurturing on their part.

Usually a series of overwhelming emotions takes place in stages upon the discovery of infidelity by one's spouse. It begins in shock and numbness that lasts anywhere from days to weeks. Sometimes the shock is so severe that the cheated spouse falls into a traumatic shock syndrome where they become separated from reality and feel as if the world around them has gone mad. Next comes denial, and then anger, which does more harm to the cheated spouse than to the spouse who committed the infidelity. Finally comes the acceptance of the horrible truth that they can never change nor forget.

The last thing caused by that traumatic event is the damage that will be felt for years to come by both spouses: the lack of trust, the bitterness, the blaming and the financial burden incurred in a divorce. Not only does the cheated spouse blame himself or herself, but their self-esteem becomes shaky or wiped out at worst. After divorce, the man will feel less adequate in approaching other females, and the woman will postpone dating for years or may never remarry.

But even if there were prior serious problems between the spouses — a lack of communication, fighting or living as strangers — there is still hope after infidelity. There is no guarantee for the partners, but they must be willing to work and resolve the new rift between them by reestablishing a stronger and lasting foundation in their marriage.

There are many excellent books that deal exclusively with life after infidelity. However, the first step is for the two partners to see a marriage counselor right away, especially for the cheated spouse, who may be going through the trauma at the initial stage. Only through communication in a therapy setting can the two partners try to resolve the crisis. In the first stage of therapy it is best for the cheated spouse to see the therapist one-on-one without the partner, to work through the repressed anger of having been cheated on; then therapy can continue with both partners present. The sessions with the therapist must be continued regularly to allow for the anger, hurt and pain to work through gradually to the stage of acceptance.

All the work of trying to cope with infidelity depends on the offending spouse coming to grips with their actions and recognizing the damage they have done to their partner and to themselves. All said and done, the cheating spouse has to make amends and undo the damage by attending the counseling sessions and nurturing the cheated spouse. This nurturing can begin with the offending partner saying to the other partner that they made a terrible mistake but they had no intention of hurting him or her, and expressing the wish to continue their married life together and their willingness to do everything in their power to make amends.

If both partners agree to work together with a verbalized agreement, then a healing can begin. Once the partners vow to show their love to each other from now on, and commit to never allowing this mistake to happen again in their marriage, then this marriage has good odds of continuing for the lifetime of the spouses.

How Men and Women View Their Spouse as a Parent

In Chapter 6 we discussed ego defense mechanisms and how we often deal with conflicts by repressing them. Those defense mechanisms will set in motion the denial of a problem or a loss. One defense mechanism I would like to discuss here is displacement. As you remember, displacement is a transference of feelings or emotions you have toward one person onto someone else. A man views his wife as the cherished woman in his life above all others, and that includes his own mother. He therefore transfers the love he has for his mother to his wife. That, however, may initiate conflict. How can he cease loving the only woman he loved as a child? This is when the line between a mother and a wife can become blurry for some individuals. That blurring is triggered by conflicts of loyalty that result from displacing love for a mother onto the wife. I call it the "mother displacement syndrome." That syndrome becomes especially pronounced the moment a woman gives birth and becomes a mother. Some men go so far as to call their wives "Mother."

What implication does this transference of the "mother" syndrome have on the marriage? A man may subconsciously feel doubts such as: "How can I view my wife as a sexual partner now that she is a mother?" Some men subconsciously believe that a woman ceases to be sexually attractive at the moment she becomes a mother. Have you ever heard a man inadvertently call his wife "Mother" when he meant to call her by her own name? I once witnessed this type of displacement firsthand in a doctor's reception room. A man well into his fifties looked in his wallet for information and said to the receptionist: "I'll call my mother...huh...my wife for the data." He caught himself saying "mother," then smiled, aware of the slip. These slips occur when the identity is blurred between the wife and the mother. After all, we grow up seeing our mothers cooking, taking care of us and loving us, the same thing that a wife does. It's no wonder that a man can come to view his wife as his mother.

A word to the man: The best way to avoid displacing attitudes toward your mother onto your wife is to set limits on the expectations you have of your wife. One way to do this is to become independent of your wife in taking care of your immediate needs; know where things are in the household, where your personal items are or paperwork pertaining to household finance. There is nothing more annoying to a wife than to have to tell her husband where to find his belt, a new bar of soap or misplaced keys. It is difficult for a wife to assume the role of a clairvoyant. A woman can be all things to her man — a companion, a wife and a mother to his children — but she cannot and should not be his mental secretary. Part of the reason for this wife/mother confusion is that mothers take responsibility for all of their child's needs. Even as adults, bachelor men rely heavily on their mothers for most of their needs when living at home with their parents. In other words, nothing changes for them when they marry nor is there a transition of attitudes for the young male when he reaches adulthood. Taking charge of one's needs as an adult means taking responsibility for oneself.

There is a wise passage dating from the year 1300 BC, in the New Kingdom of ancient Egypt, quoted in the book *Mistress of the House, Mistress of Heaven*. In this passage a man has written a letter of instructions to his son telling him what a husband should do in regard to his wife (Capel, Markoe & Bryan, 1996):

> Do not control your wife in her house when you know that she is efficient. Don't say to her, "Where is it? Get it!" when she has put it in the right place. Let your eyes observe in silence for then you'll recognize her skill. It is joy when your hand is with her. There are many who don't know this. If a man desists from strife at home, he will not encounter its beginning. Every man who founds a household should hold back a hasty heart. *

This blurring of a parent with a spouse also applies to a woman. A woman may call her husband "Daddy" and displace affection for her father onto her husband. In addition, a woman may expect from her husband the same treatment she received at home from her father. We know how easy it is for a father to give in to "Daddy's girl." Daddy's girl can do no wrong. Daddy's girl will know that fact from childhood and subconsciously apply this pattern when requesting favors from her husband. Parents can also add to the complexity of family attachments by subconsciously treating their children as surrogates for a spouse when their own spouse is unavailable or non-existent.

Exercise 16: Realistic Expectations I Have of My Spouse.

This exercise should be done by both spouses individually: In your journal you will list the expectations you have of your spouse and the expectations you had of your parents when you were a child or young adult. Look honestly at how you displace your feelings toward your parents onto your spouse. List your expectations in three columns: one for your father, one for your mother, and one for your spouse. (See the example given in the next chart.) In the first two columns put down the expectations you had as a child for each parent. In the third column put down at least ten of the adult expectations you have of your spouse.

When you have finished, see if any expectations are the same across columns. Now cross out all the expectations in your parents' columns, leaving only the expectations you have of your spouse. If any expectations in you spouse's column match childhood expectations you had in your parents' columns, cross those out too, except for expectations that are normal and realistic in adulthood. For example, in the column of the chart, "Nurturing," "Be there for me" and "Play with me" can be left in, but "feed and serve me" should be crossed out. "Financial support" can be a decision that rests with the partners and the expendable income one spouse can provide for the other. Transfer the remaining expectations in your spouse's column onto an index card and title it "Realistic Expectations I Have of My Spouse."

Expectations of My Parents and My Spouse

Expectations I Had of My Father	Expectations I Had of My Mother	Expectations I Have of My Spouse
Financial Support.	Nurturing.	Financial support and nurturing.
Be there for me.	Be there for me.	Be there for me.
Play with me.	Feed and serve me.	Play with me and feed and serve me.

Both men and women have the inherent capacity to love and accept love. This capacity for love is the soft and tender side of our nature that each one of us possesses. When a man closes the door on nurturing his life and others' lives, or shuts down the feminine side of his mind and nature and instead focuses exclusively on his manly side, he has short-changed himself. He has closed the door of this part of humanity within him that can make him respond to a woman's touch and fully enjoy the gifts that a woman brings. The same applies to the woman. If she ceases to develop the masculine side of her nature where, besides nurturing life, she can make her own decisions on the quality she wants for her life, she cannot envision a man's viewpoint or aspirations in life. The unification, rather than separation, of the masculine and feminine parts of our nature is what elevates us to a higher plane of consciousness.

Exercise Progress

By now you have completed all of the exercises through number 16. You now have working tools ranging from merging to introspection, from fulfilling your partner's needs to stopping destructive thought patterns, and can see yourself and your partner as equal powers behind the success in your marriage. Keep a consistent time schedule for exercises. They can be in the morning when your mind is fresh, or at the end of the day when work is no longer interfering with these goal-oriented activities to improve your marriage. Keep in mind that these exercises are like mason's bricks — each stone will build upon the next until your home is standing upright.

Conclusion

On the path to the blissful marriage, at the top of the list in Capital letters is COMMITMENT. Once this sacred word is written and verbalized, there is no veering away. Next is the imbued sense that this *marriage* is not a trap but rather a *trophy* that will bring not only admiration from others but also respect for its longevity. Staying married is akin to building the *Rock of Gibraltar*, while divorces are the storms that wreck coastlines and lives — the homes can be rebuilt but lives will be lost forever. A key word is *faithfulness*. Without this trust no marriage will survive. Adding to the scars of unfaithfulness is a loss of security for the other partner — constant doubts and the unsettling feeling that the danger and threat will always be there. Another solid word is *reality*. We tend to live in an unreal world made up by the media, Hollywood, dollar signs and fake beings. This influence, not unlike imprinting in the critical years of childhood, can impress upon young minds and in adulthood that this is the norm. We are daily fed a diet of so-called values: such as: be young, be thin, be beautiful, be muscular and have tight buns, be super intelligent, be fast, be, be, be...With each subliminal order given, as though by a circus trainer, we submissively absorb the messages and jump to perform accordingly. This willingness to obey those suggestions without questioning is what causes us to lose our uniqueness and blend in with the crowd. This unreal world contributes to cracks and stresses in the marriage. Instead, by listening to our *own voice*, the voice of preservation and reason, we can find *true happiness* in a marriage made both on earth and in heaven.

— 10 —

Putting Order in Your Life

I have found a delicate wave-green solitude.
Here, in the fairy wood, between sea and sea,
I have heard the song of a fairy bird in a tree,
And the peace that is not in the world has flown to me.

—Arthur Symons

Have you ever said to yourself, "I have grown tired of all the mess, the hardships, the arguments and the whole shebang"? Of course you have. You would not be human if you did not address those questions occasionally. From time to time we all stop to reflect on our lives. Human beings have the capacity to probe, analyze, rationalize, make errors, then correct them as they go through life. We learned to shape our environment in infancy by alerting our caregivers with our cries that hunger was stirring within us. We then gained confidence when the caregiver responded and we learned that somehow we controlled our environment. Cries of hunger, frustration, fear, pain and delight were all part of our repertoire to attract attention, control our environment and get results as we were growing up.

These primitive human emotions are triggered whenever we stumble or face a wall. If we think back, we can all remember something we wanted so badly, and when we did not get it we reacted with supplication, coaxing, anger or rage. When that object of desire still was not delivered to our doorstep we may have retreated into sulking, not talking or being plain moody.

As adults, we do the same today except that those emotions range farther in complexity. Depression or self-abuse is one form of expressing that we have not had our wishes or needs granted. Illnesses from frustrated needs can range from ulcers or migraine headaches, to sleep-lessness or despondency. Some of these illnesses can also stem from biological disturbances, so they should be checked out first by a qualified physician.

The body has a strange ability to send signals when all is not well with our emotional makeup or psyche. A constant disregard of such vital needs as love, affection or sex can degenerate into emotional illnesses that may manifest themselves as physical. A psychological illness can breed recurring biological ailments and disease in the body. This can occur when the brain has encoded an unfulfilled need as an ailment in the body. Only a discerning physician can separate the biological from the psychological causes. Other examples of psychological illnesses can be allergies and rashes, and suppression of the immune system which can leave one vulnerable to a number of diseases.

Dealing with Stress

One of the great instigators of life's illnesses is stress. Stress is a number one killer. The stresses of everyday life might include losing a job, marital conflict, fear of crime and disease, fear of becoming poor or abandoned and even reaching a goal, to name a few. To understand what stress can do to the human body, let us turn to a brief explanation of the body's ability to fend off stress.

Stress is defined in Neil Carlson's *Foundations of Physiological Psychology* as "the physiological reaction caused by the perception of aversive or threatening situations." A person's health can become affected when negative emotions build up as a result of aversive stimuli.

To understand how aversive stimuli affect our health, let us look at the highest-functioning part of our central nervous system, the brain. The brain contains three interconnected chambers: the forebrain, the midbrain, and the hindbrain. These three important parts of the brain, composed of neurons or nerve cells, receive information from the environment and transmit neural impulses. This allows us to think, move our muscles, and sense the world around us through sight, sound, and smell.

In the forebrain is found the cerebral cortex, the convoluted part of the brain that looks somewhat like the intestines. Right below the forebrain is an important cell structure called the *hypothalamus*, which is involved in fighting, feeding, fleeing and mating. These emotional responses were designed to equip us with the fight-or-flight mode of reacting for the survival of our species. A certain amount of stress or negative emotion is therefore beneficial to prepare us to fend off or flee from danger. The role of the hypothalamus in this survival is to regulate the autonomic (meaning: self-governing) nervous system that controls adrenal glands, cardiac and smooth muscles. When the adrenal glands (found on top of the kidneys) become stimulated by the hypothalamus in response to danger, stress hormones are secreted along with increased blood flow and glucose (carbohydrates converted to sugar) in preparation for strenuous activity.

As the body reacts to a short-term stressful episode the increase in blood flow, stress hormones and glucose prepares us for the event, and then the body returns to normal activity. In long-term stressful events, however, prolonged stress hormone secretions and continuous heart rate overactivity with an increase in blood flow are harmful. Some of the harmful effects of prolonged stress are cardiovascular diseases with an increase in blood pressure that can lead to strokes and heart attacks. Steroid diabetes, growth inhibition, infertility, and suppression of the immune system, which increases vulnerability to infectious diseases, can also be brought on by prolonged stress (Carlson, 1995).

The harmful effects of stress are made worse by our perception of that stress. In other words, it is how we perceive a threatening event that can affect us the most. As we saw in Chapter 5, our perceptions and beliefs can lead us to misinterpret another person's intentions and become emotionally upset. Stress can also have the same effect when we perceive a constant danger to our being or integrity. We know right away when we face real danger, but a perceived threatening situation is more subtle. It is one where we feel we have no control over a situation, and that feeling of powerlessness is what adds to the stress. For example, if your supervisor at work is using dishonest tactics to have you demoted or to withhold a raise, then this is a stressful situation where you have no control. Even if you are willing to denounce the management at the expense of your position, either way you will be exposed to a stressful situation. And if you don't know how to deal with the stress, it then becomes exponential until it makes you ill.

For example, I once found myself in one of those situations when I was working in a small office. My desk was very close to other clerks' desks, and when my phone rang (sometimes with other phones ringing simultaneously) I could barely hear the caller at the other end of the line. I was suffering at that time from constant noise stress, and additionally, I was picking up the flu and colds from other workers in that small space from using the same typewriters and other office machines. Within four months I came down with colds, then bronchitis, then another cold and so on. My immune system was shot because I didn't know how to deal with the stress in that office.

Some situations may stress one individual and not another. How a person perceives a negative event influences how they will react and cope with that event. Stressful situations in a marriage can occur as a result of misunderstandings, denial of existing problems, and the way we perceive our partner's words or thought process. Clearing up misunderstandings and having control over a difficult situation can reduce stress and enhance a relationship. The first step in eliminating a stressful situation is to ask yourself some questions: "Is this situation truly harmful to my well-being, or am I only perceiving it as a threat? How can I eliminate a stressor, or improve a negative situation? Am I being overreactive and over-emotional about trifles, or is this really a very stressful situation?" By first asking these questions you have already eliminated the anxiety of a vague nagging feeling. You should always take the proper steps to resolve a situation that is dangerous to your well-being. Physical harm and verbal and emotional abuse are real and need immediate attention.

If the stressful situation is a spouse who is inattentive, alienated or depressed, then you need to merge with your spouse's psyche and ask yourself why he or she is in that emotional mode. You need to ask your spouse why he or she is quiet, non-responsive or unavailable to you. These questions should be asked in a caring, low-toned voice if possible. Questions asked in an accusatory or high-pitched tone of voice will put your partner in an automatic self-defense mode and might deepen their depression. When you ask your spouse those questions, you can also let them know how you feel as a result of their lack of communication. You can tell them that you feel isolated by their silence and miss their companionship. This line of two-way communication will lower the stress and reestablish the loving relationship you have for each other.

Unfulfilled needs in our lives will overwhelm our brain by focusing our attention and efforts only in one area, and that will take away precious energy needed for the body to function. Visualize the brain for a moment as a main center for distribution. This center or headquarters coordinates the whole body's system of cells and organs. If that center becomes overstressed, then the whole system is affected. Now picture the brain being overwhelmed with anxiety, which in turns releases too much adrenaline, stress hormones or acid in the body. This constant stress on the body can cause ailments such as ulcers or hypertension.

To eliminate stress in your life you need to prioritize; you need to reason and choose between the real and the imagined. You do that by introspection and merging with that person you love. You need to ask yourself: "Who is the most important person in my life? How can I improve my life and my spouse's life? What are my real goals in life? Am I striving to achieve those goals to please or impress others, or is this a real sense of duty that motivates me? How can I achieve those goals without sacrificing my personal relationship with my spouse?"

Providing for Your Needs

The first thing you need to do in providing for your needs is to create a strategy. You will first ask yourself, what are the stumbling blocks in your marriage or relationship, and then draw out a plan for eliminating them. Next you need to take each stumbling block and apply various solutions to improve or eliminate the conflict.

For example, if the conflict is that your spouse is often late for dinner, then you need to sit down with your spouse and discuss how that affects you. You can communicate how lonely it is for you to eat alone and how you would like to be with him or her in sharing a meal. Find alternate ways to deal with the problem. You might join your spouse at his or her workplace and have a light meal together in the office or at a nearby restaurant. Many companies allow family members to join employees on their lunch or dinner hour. The whole family sharing dinner every night is less common these days than in the days of Ozzie and Harriet in the 1950s. Surveys have discovered, though, that families who eat their meals together are better adjusted and closer emotionally. At the dinner table conversations can pivot around the day's events, and each person can communicate vital information to other family members who can offer support and validate their experience.

Another way to provide for your needs is to visualize how much better off you would be if you put your plans into action. For example, if you are at a dead end in your job then you need to draw up plans and discuss with your spouse alternative ways to improve your work prospects. Your spouse will then merge with your predicament and offer support and solutions. Together you will come up with the ideal plan to improve your career. Do not wait until anxiety and stress get the better of you and induce illness in your body and mind. As soon as you eliminate the conflicts in your own life, your married life will take a more sure course on the path to bliss.

The humanistic psychologist Abraham Maslow theorized that when each level of needs is successively fulfilled, an individual reaches self-actualization, the highest level of functioning one can attain. These needs, placed in hierarchical levels, lead to the apex of self-actualization:

Abraham Maslow's Self-Actualization Needs

Highest	Need for Self-Actualization: To become the best one can be.
	Esteem Needs: Adequacy, self-respect, competence and mastery.
	Belongingness and Love Needs: Roots for family and peers, affection and intimacy.
	Safety Needs: Security; avoidance of pain and anxiety.
Lowest	Physiological Needs: Protection from hunger, thirst and fatigue.

Reprinted by permission from *Beneath the Mask* by Christopher F. Monte, 1994.

These needs are innate in every individual. The higher needs cannot be reached until the lower needs have been satisfied. Therefore, the physiological needs must be satisfied before an individual can go on to meeting the next higher level, the safety needs. Belongingness and love needs must be met, otherwise esteem needs will suffer lack of fulfillment. I have met many individuals who struggle for a lifetime to achieve their goals. They reach a certain level but are not able to finish and put that goal in motion. Their belongingness and love needs were either at a standstill or were lacking altogether. These individuals suffer from being "directionless."

Prioritizing Duties

Another way to improve your married life is to be self-sufficient and independent in the small tasks of everyday living. These can include the various duties that married life brings, such as household chores, financial duties, childrearing, and family responsibilities. Those responsibilities can become overwhelming and induce more stress unless they are distributed in an orderly fashion.

To accomplish these tasks and share equally in these necessary duties it helps to write them down and put the list on your refrigerator door. Rotating these tasks is also beneficial so you don't become stale in one area. These household duties have to be carried out to the letter, otherwise chaos will follow. Have you ever seen a corporation asking their employees to do their jobs as they pleased? That corporation wouldn't be in business for very long. It is equally true that we live in a world full of rules, regulations and commandments, but without these rules no order could reign.

One way to eliminate overwhelming and unnecessary duties is to say NO to them. This is of the utmost importance to our mental and physical well-being. You can learn to say NO without guilt by setting priorities. You can begin by making a list of your existing duties to people and organizations. After you draft this list, select those duties you wish by assigning them an order of importance and eliminating the ones with no redeeming benefit to you personally. When we go by the old adage of "Charity begins at home," we can be sure of who and what is important to us. Expending our energy on a number of charitable institutions at the expense of our loved ones is not charitable. We then need to ask ourselves, "Why am I spending so much time helping others when my spouse needs my help even more? Why do I need outside validation when my spouse is the one I really need?" Our need for love and intimacy can sometimes drive us to distraction and to the point of exhaustion. By focusing our priorities, we can then expend our energies where they are needed most.

Being True to Ourselves

Other stumbling blocks to a blissful marriage are the burdens and shackles of lifestyles that we impose upon ourselves when we blindly follow the subtle messages of commercialism. We need to see through the veneer of materialism imposed on us by billboards, magazine ads and the like in order to be true to ourselves. We can do that by being selective and by discerning our real self from our false self. Our real self is better served, for example, by exercise or joining a gym to improve our health and appearance. On the other hand, becoming obsessed with exercise to the point of wanting to mold our body into something that it is not is addictive, and that shackles us with a false self. It is estimated that nearly 10 million women suffer from crash diets, bulimia, anorexia and unnecessary surgery to mold themselves into images projected by the fashion and movie industries. The noted author Sue Bender was mentioning in her book *Everyday Sacred*, that she had told her agent, Mitzi, she wouldn't hand in her manuscript until it was perfect. Her agent then replied, "The best of what we are is more than enough." We need to set boundaries for our body and mind to prevent outside interference from changing who we really are.

Who we are *is* enough. This package we come with is our true self. To change who we really are is to invite personality conflicts that may last a lifetime. After all our self-imposed physical changes, we will still be searching for our true identity. We have the power to be our true selves, and by not giving away or "selling out" this power we have control over our lives. It is when life is free of conflict and dependence that we flow toward a betterment of ourselves, and only then can we be free to look toward others and the future.

Exercise 17: How to Serve My Loved Ones

Turn now to your journal and list all the obligations you have. Number them in order of importance and cross out the unnecessary obligations and addictive burdens. They are superfluous if they take time away from your spouse and family. Then transfer them onto an index card and title it "How to Serve My Loved Ones."

Conclusion

Nothing can replace the warm emotional feeling of a close relationship to your spouse. This close relationship is to be *honored* and *respected*. We preserve our *true self* by not compromising who we really are with false self-imposed lifestyles. This prevents and frees us from adverse stress that can make us ill. We can also eliminate a stressful situation by distinguishing between a perceived harm and a real danger to our being. Learn to say NO without guilt when you become overburdened with unnecessary duties. We alleviate this load by focusing on our relationship, and by the *prioritization* of duties. This *strategy* and *two-way communication* can then clear up conflicts and reestablish the loving relationship you have for each other. Once we focus and let our vital energies flow we can then move up the *scale* of *needs* and *self-growth* until we become *self-actualized*. As we reach this pinnacle of human needs we then find *truth* and *beauty* in our lives.

Part II
THE CATERPILLAR

— 11 —

The Middle
Years: 30-55

Seize this day, this moment.
It is here only once,
and will never
be here again..

In the middle of our married lives we suddenly come to the realization that we cannot catch up on lost years. We then begin to look back and regret the elapsed years. It is a time when we feel that lost opportunities may not arise again or that we may be past an age for some ventures in life. This is a time when, against our will, we may become unfocused and distracted in our true quest in life: love and self-actualization. Remember that being loved is not what we have accomplished in the past or how influential we can be. Love is having the freedom to be who we really are.

Merging with Your Parents

At this time in your life you are at a comparable age with your parents when they began to look back on their past. You can now experience some of their regrets, their unfulfilled dreams and disappointments. This is the time to merge with your parents and to set aside all the rancor you have. If they were not there for you or unable to satisfy your needs, you can turn to your children (if you have any) and see if you are satisfying their needs. If you have been there for them, it means that you are satisfied with your lot in life and are focusing on guiding their steps. If that is the case, you are a fortunate individual. Dissatisfied parents cannot be there for their children if they are still trying to fulfill their own childhood or young adulthood dreams.

Now turn back the clock, go back in time and put yourself in your parents' lives. Merge with your parents and feel their disappointments, their struggles and their losses, as not much different from your own. Considering this scenario, could your parents have focused on your needs when their energy was used up entirely on chasing their own dreams? If they were fortunate enough to have had someone who cared and pointed the way for them, then you would today be in an advantageous place. Since multi-generational dysfunction often lasts for three or four generations, you have the option to put a stop to all the grief and unhappiness by declaring yourself free from it all. You have this power and free will to choose to be broken and hurt, or to experience the joys of living. Since no one can turn back the clock and undo the past, we may as well enjoy the present. You can say to yourself: "If I do not live these next five minutes fully they will become part of the past and can never come back."

Career and the Family

Spending time with one's spouse and getting close to each other can become an elusive pursuit in many marriages, to say the least. Careers and professions take exceptional amounts of time and workers often find themselves married to their jobs. These jobs can take the form of an escape or become obsessional. That is when the marriage will suffer from alienation and the loss of companionship for the other spouse.

Whenever we find ourselves spending too much time on one activity to the exclusion of others, we then know it is obsessional and needs to be evaluated. How do we know when work or some other occupation becomes an obsession? It is when we work ten to fifteen hours a day, every day, for long periods of time. We rationalize that the job must be finished on time, or we procrastinate then have no option but to work around the clock. This form of obsessional activity can often be a distraction from thoughts that our ego found unacceptable to deal with. You can go back to Chapter 6 and review the ego defense mechanisms that occur when unacceptable impulses are repressed into the unconscious. See if any of these defense mechanisms apply to you, and if so, how you can deal with it. For what reasons have you become engrossed in your work or other activity? Analyze when this overactivity first took place. Was it before a significant incident in your life? Did a traumatic experience or event occur at about the same time? No human being can give or sustain excessive amounts of energy to an activity devoid of feelings and emotions.

Let's assume that while overextending your energies and burying yourself in work, you were also, and with the best of intentions, in the process of amassing wealth. It cannot, however, give you the warmth and loving feelings you would get from spending time with your spouse and children. Every moment invested in your loved ones gives you incomparable returns. Think for a moment of the advantages. Your spouse can experience your presence, your affection and love, and communication that occurs between the two of you. In return your partner will be receptive to your needs and strive for your happiness. Your children can communicate to you their needs, joys or disappointments. You are there for all of them. These moments are precious and can never be there again. The clock does not stop for your loved ones while you are buried in work. Time goes on ticking for them, and their loss is cumulative with each minute.

Curtailing work and career activities for your family's sake is a sacrifice that you make for them. The time invested in nourishing your partner and children will bring unequaled returns, better than any monetary results. We can always rationalize that the extra work is done for our loved ones, that they will enjoy these returns. But ask your spouse or child these questions and see what their answer is. In every case they will prefer your presence to any new toy or material possession. The time you spend in holding their hand, stroking your spouse's back or bringing your spouse a cup of coffee in the morning is invaluable. The time you spend with your children on the playground is better than any new gadget on the market.

Families who make time for at least one meal a day together and one day on the weekend are found to be better adjusted than most. The quality of that time together is also critical. Communication becomes greatly reduced when parents or children spend great amounts of time watching television or at the computer. Family gatherings instill a sense of safety, joy and the comfort that we belong and have continuity.

Dreams and the Future

One of the hardest things in life is to let go of unrealistic dreams. Sometimes even realistic aspirations need to be put on hold temporarily so that we can focus on the present in order to build the future. Imagine for a moment how you want your future to be. You could then put into action (with written plans) how you would design that future. How can you plan your future without compromising the present?

You begin by letting go. You let go of the "I could have done this" or "I should have done that." You let go of unfinished business: childhood dreams, settling scores or getting back at someone for insults. You forgive. The power of forgiveness is greater than anything imaginable. To forgive someone for something done to you is close to having the power of a God. It gives us the power of magnanimity. If I can forgive, then I am powerful. We can forgive our parents for not satisfying our needs when we were small, and for being human and full of dreams just like us. We can also let go by declaring our free will and not being bound to anything that would compromise our life, integrity or freedom.

Between thirty and forty years of age we reach a pinnacle of experiences not realized in our youth. We have unbounded energy when young and experience when older, and learn about life as we go. We take on new jobs, projects and activities to match the extent of our health and energy. If you are now in your thirties or forties, visualize how your future might be depending on how you spend your working hours or free time now.

To plan a future takes not only foresight but also the vision to see yourself in that place. Let's say, for example, that at the age of retirement, at about sixty-two, you want to have the financial means to live comfortably and be able to travel with your spouse. It is when you strive with that goal in mind that the future will happen. To make this dream happen you need your partner's presence, proximity, help and harmonious communication. When two people work together toward their future they become partners in their life continuity.

Now if you roll back the years to your mid-thirties, think of any characteristics you have that could become obstacles in your way. For example, think about the sexual power and vitality we have during those years. This sometimes explosive sexual drive can lead us to expend it without control or selectiveness. It can lead us to use it indiscriminately, so that it becomes a weapon turned against us. Instead, that drive can be channeled into the marriage so that we experience heights of love and ecstasy. This can happen if we work on the marriage relationship to let us in through this golden door. When two people are committed and work for the betterment of the marriage relationship, sex becomes one of the highest peak experiences of your life. This height of experience can only be reached if both spouses allow each other's growth. It is by achieving a blissful relationship in the present that we can experience and fulfill most of our dreams in the future.

You need to ask yourself, what is presently the roadblock in my marriage and my future? For each individual these hurdles can be different. Some of those wrong turns can lead you to be unfocused. For example, you could be chasing unrealistic dreams. You could be spending some savings on feeding those dreams. Other ways of diverging from your true goals in life are "romantic" or emotional ventures outside your marriage. These ventures can also fall into the category of unrealistic dreams: chasing the perfect woman or man that will give you this unattainable love you have been searching for all your life. Again these remain dreams. They have no substance nor can they add building stones to your future. Remember that when these roadblocks occur it is because we operate under the belief that we were not loved as a child. Therefore, we make the wrong assumption that we are not loved by our spouse, and that only this fascinating stranger will make it all right for us. This feeling of being unloved belongs in the past. It moves with you throughout life and when it resurfaces it may create pain for you. When that seemingly magnetic stranger becomes the focus of your love life, you need to ask yourself, how can a stranger love me more than my spouse? How can she or he know my most secret desires, know my likes and dislike of little things in life, and how can they attend to those needs? Ten times out of ten this stranger is just that: one who is not committed to your needs or interests in life. This stranger is detrimental to your well-being and their presence stops the clock for you and your spouse.

Whenever we turn away from our true course in life we begin an unraveling. This unraveling stems from old destructive habits rooted in the belief that we are unlovable. We believe that no one wants us or loves us, and this is a time when we stop growing. Growing is a process that leads ever forward in a positive direction. Your growth should always be the primary motivation in your life. Whenever you become unfocused you stop growing, and so does your spouse. A husband or wife becoming emotionally un-available instills anxiety in the marriage. That anxiety will bring stress and disharmony into that marriage. This then, is a time when the clock stops and there is no present or future for either one of you.

The first step in preventing roadblocks when planning for the future is to design a realistic plan for where both of you want to be five years from now, ten years, fifteen, and so on. How are you going to tackle this plan and how much capital will it take? Give each other feedback on your likes and dislikes for that plan. Discuss any objections and find ways to reach a compromise. You do that by using introspection about objections. Merge with your spouse and find out what in their past is standing as a roadblock to your wishes. By progressing in the mastery of merging and introspection, you will see objections and hurdles disappear. Harmony and bliss will then follow in your marriage.

Exercise 18: Our Future Plans

Take out your journal and list all the unrealistic dreams you are carrying within you. Go through each one and see how they impede your growth and your relationship with your spouse. Next make a list of realistic plans and how to start them. Have your spouse go through the same steps and compare notes on how to combine those plans to the satisfaction of both of you. Now take an index card and list the plans in order of urgency, along with their time allotment. Title this card "Our Future Plans."

Conclusion

Regrets or missed opportunities can use up vital energy you need to *love* and *self-actualize*. To be *loved* we have to be free to be *who we are*. This is a time to *forgive* and *let go*. Your *spouse* can give you *warmth* and *love*. You can never get this feeling from strangers, careers or professions. The *present* is all we have. If we do not live in the present we will erase the *future*. We then free ourselves from all the unnecessary or obsessional activities to plan this future. This released freedom will channel an unbounded energy into the marriage and contribute to *sexual ecstasy*.

— 12 —

The Great Communicators

The art of communication leads to the art of living and loving well.

A two-way, flowing communication between two human beings is the spark that enhances a marriage. This communication flow is like a stream that smooths and polishes the stones on its way and reflects the light of the sun. Without a two-way communication between adults, we would not know who we are with others, but would live as an island onto ourselves. Communication is not only exchanging words and ideas, it is also revealing our innermost thoughts, the essence of who we are. In revealing our souls there is also the fear of criticism, or being reprimanded, diminished or wounded. That is why many of us remain aloof, uncommunicative or plain deaf. Instead, if we could communicate our thoughts, requests and needs in a safe and encouraging atmosphere, we would release those long-repressed thoughts and desires. How can we express ourselves without having this sword of Damocles above our heads? This chapter on communication will explain the how of smooth-flowing dialogue between two partners.

The various workshops on the communicative skills of listening emphasize the major points of successful dialogues: choice words, non-judgmental listening, respectful listening, accepting that there are many viewpoints besides your own, and a non-bullying attitude. In addition, there are specific techniques that focus on improving communication by avoiding repetitive sentences, too much or too little information given, and stonewalling. The tools most needed when two partners are locked in conflictual issues are merging, empathic listening, verbalizing feelings, introspection and examining irrational beliefs.

A sure way to the divorce court is to stand your ground stubbornly without giving an inch or listening to your spouse. When you stand your ground to be listened to, express your feelings but then listen to the response without interruption. If you receive information contrary to your wishes, you can then re-express your point of view with a more explicit request. Again, you need to view communication as an exchange of views and information. It is not a contest of wills on who can win in the end. Each partner puts forward their viewpoint while taking into consideration the other's view. This flowing exchange of two-way information leads to growth and love.

The simplest exchanges of information between two partners can sometimes become misconstrued and stunted if important elements such as merging, analyzing your own irrational beliefs and verbalizing feelings are swept aside. Without these constructive elements, you only talk and reply without developing and building communication that enhances relationships. In the next pages you will find examples contrasting stunted and constructive communication: diverging vs. converging, non-empathic vs. empathic, and attack vs. peaceful communications.

Diverging Communication

In diverging communication, both spouses focus on their own needs without listening to one another:

Request for Empathy	Non-Listening
Jean: Today I had a bad headache. The kids yelled the whole time I was shopping, and I've been too exhausted to make dinner.	*Rick:* I told you before, don't take the kids with you when you're shopping. Now we have no dinner!
Jean: I knew I couldn't count on you!	*Rick:* You're never happy!

This exchange between Jean and Rick was not productive, nor did it alleviate Jean's feeling of helplessness with the day's events. Rick used this exchange as a chance to assert his authority with the "I told you ..." statement. Rick also felt that he was put on the spot. Rick interpreted Jean's complaint as an accusation that it's his fault Jean is stuck with responsibility for the kids, and he felt that he had to "fix" the situation (an irrational belief). Jean did not request Rick's help, but waited for him to read her mind. So Jean's need for empathy was not met and now she is in no state to make dinner for all of them.

Converging Communication

In converging communication, one spouse is communicating and the other is listening and empathizing.

Request for Empathy	Merging and Listening
Pat: Today I had a bad headache. The kids yelled the whole time I was shopping, and I've been too exhausted to make dinner.	*Tom:* (thinking to himself, Pat looks beat.) Honey, why don't you lie down. I'll give the kids a light dinner then we'll eat later.

Request for Empathy	Merging and Listening
Pat: Thanks, Honey. I'll fix something good for us later. I love you, babe.	*Tom*: (thinking , that's my romantic gal) I love you too.

Communication between individuals is more than conveying information and viewpoints. It consists of verbalizing feelings and can be emotionally charged with cries for help. Do not confuse a cry for empathy and help with a demand or command. This is not the army and we are not expected to deliver on command. Ninety-five percent of the time a cry for help is a need to be listened to and validated.

Here are some suggestions that can facilitate communication with your spouse or other loved ones:

- Let them finish their sentences.
- Give them time to express their discomfort.
- Cooperate with their requests.
- Respect their views.
- Listen with attentiveness.
- Empathize with their feelings of helplessness.
- Be non-judgmental in your comments or replies.
- Do not be defensive.
- Do not rush to offer a remedy until you have heard the request.
- Above all, do not play the blame game or the being blamed game.

Most of the time when a partner expresses discomfort, hurt feelings or pain, it is not done to blame but rather to simply express their hurt.

Always watch out for criticism in your voice, a loud tone of voice, attack and counterattack attitudes, finger-pointing, blackmail, defensiveness, manipulation and changing the subject. These tactics are sticks of dynamite that can destroy a marriage.

Non-Empathic Communication

In non-empathic communication one partner is expressing feelings and pain while the other spouse automatically goes on the defensive and is not able to listen.

Pain and Confusion	Defensiveness and Non-Listening
Rick: I can't believe how you embarrassed me in front of Tina and Mark by saying that I don't take you out.	*Jean*: (raising her voice) You're so sensitive! I was only sympathizing with Tina for the same reason.
Rick: Even so, I was mortified! Mark will tell everyone at work!	*Jean*: You're always afraid of what your co-workers are thinking.
Rick: (angry) Oh, I give up!	*Jean*: So do I.

This discussion could have been more productive if Jean had used more empathy for Rick's feelings. Jean went into an automatic defense mode when the blame was directed at her. She did not merge with Rick to feel his embarrassment and discomfort (a man automatically feels responsible for his wife's well-being, and that includes entertainment). Besides feeling embarrassed in front of his friends, Rick could not get his message across to Jean. They had reached an impasse with non-communicative dialogue.

Empathic Communication

In empathic communication, one spouse is expressing hurt while the other spouse is listening and merging with the pain they inadvertently caused.

Pain and Confusion	Merging and Empathic Listening
Tom: I can't believe how you embarrassed me in front of Tina and Mark by saying that I don't take you out.	*Pat*: (in a soft voice) I'm sorry I embarrassed you. In my sympathy for Tina I neglected your feelings. I'm sorry I put you through this.
Tom: I'm glad you understand.	*Pat*: How can I make it up to you?
Tom: How about a romantic dinner tonight?	*Pat*: This one will be special!

To tune in to Tom's embarrassment and discomfort at being criticized in front of his friends, Pat used merging and listening. Next, she verbally acknowledged Tom's pain by saying how sorry she was. Tom's anger at Pat cooled down when his feelings were validated and he was glad that she understood him. The romantic dinner suggestion is the icing on the cake.

When couples argue about money, children's up-bringing, and especially sex, it's not because they do not want or love each other. The arguments and breakdown in communication happen because each one feels responsible for the other and assumes the blame for having failed. Both partners also have expectations of each other and when they go unfulfilled, disappointment sets in.

Attack Communication

With attack communication, the immediate perception of one partner is that it's entirely the other person's fault for having created the problem.

Call for Help	Blame and Non-Listening
Jean: Our bills are humongous! You need to watch your spending. It's all this software you're buying!	*Rick*: (raising his voice) Look who's talking! What about that dress you just bought?
Jean: (upset) I haven't bought a dress in ages!	*Rick*: I don't buy clothes. I prefer software for my computer.
Jean: (angry) I can never talk to you!	*Rick*: (not budging) Go ahead, talk!

In this example both Jean and Rick were talking through each other rather than to each other. Jean's comment about Rick's expenditure was a complaint rather than a call for help. Rick, on the other hand, was using the tit-for-tat technique (you buy a dress and I buy software) when blame was directed at him. After that, Jean got off track about reducing Rick's spending and went on to defend her own spending. Rick's comment to Jean at the end exemplifies why some couples never solve problems and perpetuate dilemmas indefinitely.

Peaceful Communication

With peaceful communication each partner listens to the other and both have enough time to digest the information and come up with a solution.

Call for Help	Listening and Solving
Pat: Our bills are humongous! What can we do to reduce spending?	*Tom*: How about cutting down on clothes and software for three months?
Pat: That sounds good to me. I'll make extra efforts to keep an eye on it.	*Tom*: Sounds good to me too. I'm relieved we solved this one!

This time Pat started her call for help with "What can we do?" without putting blame on Tom. By making the issue a mutual problem, Tom feels a share in the responsibility and does not feel he's the only one at fault. By not having to defend himself, Tom is able to focus on the problem and come up with a solution. Both Pat and Tom willingly cooperated to reduce spending and kept a smooth line of communication between them.

How the Brain Perceives Criticism

Whenever blame is directed by one partner to the other, the only reply is one of defense: a counterattack to shield against attack. Our brain is wired and programmed for survival. In the evolutionary climb of humankind, this survival instinct has functioned throughout many thousands of years. There are three major divisions of the brain: the forebrain, the midbrain and the hindbrain. Of those three, the forebrain, also called the "new brain," and the hindbrain, called the "old or primitive brain," are significant in communication. In the hindbrain is found the primitive, evolutionary "think tank" for the human being. The hindbrain is located behind and below the forebrain in the brain stem, the most primitive part of the brain, and is the repository of all instinctive knowledge and tactics for survival. Information in that knowledge bank helped preservation and survival by recognizing danger and food sources, and by governing reproduction and most important autonomous functions such as blood circulation, respiration and muscle movement. The new brain evolved after the old brain in the evolution of humankind. As such, the new brain is responsible for making everyday decisions that concern the visible world around us (Carlson, 1995).

As you recall from Chapter 2, our brain is programmed to receive information in milliseconds that informs us whether someone is friend or foe. The movements and gestures we perceive in another will alert our primitive brain to any danger, and that includes words and facial expressions. If our partner is acting in a way perceived as detrimental to our self or psyche, our primitive brain goes into danger mode to alert us. This danger alert can be set off by anything from frequent interruptions to actions or words carrying criticism, blame or judgmental opinions. We then react with our primitive brain and go into a self-defense mode: defending our actions, words or opinions. This perception by our primitive brain, or old brain, is regulated by the forebrain, or new brain.

In our example with Jean and Rick, Rick's old brain sends information to his new brain that Jean just blamed him for spending too much on computer software. Rick's new brain will digest the information and send it back to his self-preserving old brain. The old brain will perceive that information as an attack on Rick because the new brain told the old brain, "There is danger in them words": Jean's words, demeanor and facial expression are threatening and non-nurturing, and therefore Rick's mind perceives an attack. Rick then responds in kind by counterattack: "What about that dress you just bought!"

Physical harm, criticism, blame or being ignored by a partner or spouse can all be translated by the old brain as threatening. Often, the old brain will perceive a real or irrational threat but will not strike back in kind. In those instances, a breakdown in survival tactics has occurred. For example, an abused child will perceive the threat but will not be able to do anything to prevent it. If the caregiver is the abuser, the child will be afraid to retaliate in kind because the caregiver is also the one who feeds and clothes that child.

All these negative, threatening perceptions are retained by our old brain and remain infinitely in its recesses.

In Rick's old brain, the blame put forth by Jean was clearly a threat demanding a retaliation in kind. Now, if Rick's old brain could be reprogrammed to perceive those same blaming words by Jean with an attitude of, as the old cliché says, "Sticks and stones will break my bones but words will never hurt me," he would have the formula for non-threatening reaction. Let's use instead, a different approach by looking at the new brain and how the merging of two people can delay attack and counterattack while enhancing and improving communication.

The new brain has the capacity to reason and respond to a situation by analyzing the problem, then creating a solution. The new brain is the computer that has the software for observing, thinking, analyzing, reasoning and decision making. Sometimes, however, we let the old brain take over the new brain and we remain in an infantile or primitive state of mind. We then see only danger and threats to our well-being and do not give our new brain the chance to examine the situation. I am not talking right now of danger such as immediate physical harm or catastrophic situations. In those cases the old brain will receive the information from the new brain and will act accordingly in a "fight-or-flight" mode. But in non-life-threatening situations, the method or principle that works best is to let the new brain do its share to control the old brain's "fight-or-flight" mode.

Exercise 19: Threats vs. Merging, Merging, Merging

In your journal draw two columns. Title one column "Threats." Title the next column "Merging." Now list Jean and Rick's critical remarks (from the "Attack Communication" dialogue earlier) in the column labeled "Threats." Also add to this column past comments where you were criticized, blamed, embarrassed in public, or unfairly judged.

In the opposite column, "Merging," you will write the words "Merging, merging, merging." For every negative comment, the opposite comment will be "Merging, merging, merging." By doing so, you will give your new brain the time and the chance to analyze the situation or the words directed at you and logically make a rational response. Now title an index card "Threats vs. Merging," and condense the threatening comments to fit on the card along with the opposite response, "Merging, merging, merging." Below is an example.

Threats	Vs.	Merging
You need to watch your spending!		Merging, merging, merging
It's all this software you're buying!		Merging, merging, merging

The purpose of this exercise is to condition yourself to hold off your defensiveness by examining your spouse's critical comments as a plea for help and not so much as an attack on your being or actions. The words "merging, merging, merging," repeated quickly mentally, will give you time to thwart a counterattack. When you have mastered this technique you will be able to focus on the request being made by your spouse or partner and reach a quick solution. Use the following "Technique for Merging" to delay the old brain's fight-or-flight stance, so you can focus on the "not always stated directly" request being put to you by your spouse. What is he/she asking for? Is he/she asking for my help, my opinion, or an apology? See your partner as the one you love, and the one who needs your help. The merging technique below can help you resolve an underlying request or issue.

Technique for Merging

1. Listen attentively.

2. Don't interrupt; delay self-defense (think "merging, merging, merging...").

3. Observe your spouse's facial expressions: irritation, anger, pain, bewilderment, a cry for help?

4. Paraphrase your spouse's comments: "You said that you want us to spend more time together in the evenings." (This reassures your partner that you are listening.) "How about if we sit down before or after dinner for a chat?"

5. Now listen to your spouse's reply. If the reply is agreeable, then you have solved the request.

6. If no compromise was reached and you have run into an impasse, set another meeting to discuss the problem the next day when the two of you are not so tired or emotionally drained.

When a Spouse Avoids Confrontation

In some communications one spouse may give in to the other to avoid a confrontation that might involve criticism, belittling, disrespectful comments or hurtful statements. These tactics usually show that the spouse is reluctant to discuss problems and instead uses a "change the subject" approach. For example, Connie did not want to discuss why she disliked having her elderly in-laws visit them. On many occasions her husband, Fred, who took an active role as a son, would go out of his way to pick them up, bring them to the house, cook the meal, then drive them back home after dinner. Connie would clear the dishes, then collapse in bed. When Fred came back home she would be fast asleep. Fred brought up the issue many times that he was feeling overwhelmed, but Connie would not help or offer a solution. Their conversation went as follows:

Fred: Connie, I can't take this anymore. I need your help when my parents visit us.	*Connie*: I really have to leave for work. We'll discuss this tonight. Where are my keys?

But the discussion never took place. Connie always changed the subject and found some excuse to postpone talking about it. Fred could not follow for fear of antagonizing Connie into a temper tantrum. Fred did not know how to stand his ground in his wish to have Connie help with the dinner when his parents visited. To stand your ground is to respect your right to be heard.

Below you will find suggestions on how to stand your ground while expressing your feelings and wish to be heard.

How to Stand Your Ground

1. Get to the point. "I would like to discuss my parents' visit now." If Connie declines, Fred can set a tentative meeting without delay for the next day. If Connie evades the next meeting, then Fred needs to let Connie know that no other meeting will do.

2. Express and verbalize your feelings. "I feel overwhelmed when my parents come to visit. Let's alternate with cooking and clearing dishes. Next time I'll do the dishes."

3. Talk about yourself. "I am exhausted after cooking, picking up my parents and driving them back."

How to Stand Your Ground

4. Express your wish. "I would like very much for both of us to agree on this."

5. Don't give up.

In many instances, the reluctance to discuss problems or issues can be traced back to childhood. Communication between two spouses or between parents and child can be fraught with stress and avoidance. These characteristics of avoiding the subject can have roots in the past when your voice was not heard after repeated requests, or judgmental comments were the response to your wishes. A young woman named Christine remembered that as a child she loved singing and listening to famous singers. One day she gathered her courage and announced to her parents that she was going to become an opera singer. Her father, who had come from a poor family and had also not been listened to as a child, replied immediately, "Are you crazy!" Nevertheless, Christine rebelled against his dismissal of her ambitions and decided to go on with singing lessons. Even though Christine had a good voice, she could not discipline herself to persevere, and after three years of classical singing lessons she gave up. In Christine's subconscious she could not succeed due to her father's lack of belief in her. To this day, this vocational wish remains unfulfilled.

Your success in communicating a need, wish or request can also depend on how much you feel loved and your fear of abandonment. Your fear of someone withholding love and affection from you can also be a strong deterrent in overlooking your needs. Ironically, the more you want to save your relationship, the more reluctant you become to express your needs. This reluctance stems from not wanting to rock the boat and being afraid of repercussions such as anger, abuse, or judgmental comments directed at you. Whatever fears you harbor from the past or present, you will perpetuate this lack of communication and leave your wishes and needs unfulfilled. Better to face the storm than to continue in the misery of unfulfilled needs. Unfulfilled needs add tremendous stress to the human body and psyche, leaving you vulnerable to illness and disease.

Antagonizing Communication

Communication between two partners can be a challenging experience but can nevertheless become rewarding as you learn the right approach to communicating with a purpose. For example, when discussing problems, always watch out for facetious or acidic remarks. It is easy to get carried away and feel your power over the other person by belittling, criticizing, or diminishing their words or worth. Above all, avoid comments and words that sting and hurt. These comments may be remembered by the wounded partner and added to their subconscious tally sheet. At the slightest provocation they will spill over and cause more damage to the marriage. Following are some examples of comments to avoid.

Comments to Avoid

I told you so, over and over.	You goofed again!
Here we go again!	Stop feeling sorry for yourself.
We've been through this before.	I work hard and what do you do all day?

Learning to avoid antagonizing communication can be beneficial to a couple to keep communication flowing.

Below are examples of ways to use soothing comments instead of acidic remarks.

Avoiding Antagonizing Communication

Acidic Remarks	Soothing Comments
Toxic: You spend too much!	*Courteous*: Let's cut expenses.
Criticism: You can't manage money!	*Respect*: How can I help?
Loud voice: You know nothing!	*Soft voice*: I happen to know...
Blame: You *know* I can't eat fried foods!	*Non-blame*: I prefer non-fried foods next time.
Blackmail: If you don't help me, I won't...	*Cooperative*: I need your help for this job.
Defense: But I always help you on weekends!	*Non-defensive*: I'm sorry about last weekend.
Counterattack: You left dirty dishes too!	*Neutral*: I'll take care of those dishes.

Communication Guidelines

In any discussion of problematic issues, always keep these guidelines in mind: Listen first, do not rush to fix, allow your spouse to finish their sentence, respect their point of view, challenge both your cooperative spirits, develop an empathic ear and mind, use a non-defensive approach with non-judgmental comments, and above all, see your spouse as a human being with feelings, wishes and the unbounded capacity to love you.

By using these approaches to communication you will avoid falling into a pattern of problem issues that have no beginning or end. This happens when unresolved problems snowball, with other issues accumulating on top of them. As a result, the issue being discussed in the present may not have anything to do with the present but have its roots buried somewhere in the past. I call these problems "enigma problems."

When the joy of life has been taken out of your marriage, then it is time to review your marriage contract and consult a professional in the field of marital counseling. You can become vulnerable to stress, illness and disease when "enigma problems" are overlooked. When such problem issues arise, it is helpful to have an agreement previously written by both partners as a guideline to remind them of their commitment to the marriage. An example of such a marriage contract follows. You can add to it or draw up your own contract with guidelines that suit both of you. This marriage contract, displayed in a prominent place, will be a testament to your willingness to grow in the relationship.

A Marriage Contract

1. Our common goal in this marriage is to help each other grow and find fulfillment.

2. We will protect this marriage from harm.

3. We are partners in this relationship.

4. We will not violate each other's rights.

5. We do not own or employ each other.

6. This contract does not give us the right to abuse, bully or be disrespectful.

7. We will find harmony through commitment.

A Marriage Contract

8. We will find continuity through family bonds.

9. Together we are powerful.

10. We will walk through love.

Exercise 20: Our Marriage Contract

Together with your spouse, create your own written marriage contract, using the example above. This exercise can be a project in creativity. You can enlarge your contract and have it printed on colored paper, enliven it with rich borders, then frame it. This contract can then become your Magna Carta or Constitution, if you will, and be a centerpiece in your home. A couple I know displayed their marriage contract in their living room where friends find it to be a constant source of conversation when they visit.

Conclusion

Communication with purpose between two people in love becomes a *flowing source* that brings meaning to the marriage. You can communicate your wishes in an atmosphere of *safety* and *encouragement*. When communicating, use the *merging technique*. Listen with *empathy*, use *courtesy* , and *respect* their opinion. All replies should be *non-judgmental* and *without blame*. If you listen carefully you can hear their *cry for help*, then act accordingly. If you wound your partner, acknowledge their pain by *undoing the hurt*. Verbalize your feelings and communicate your request in two-way dialogues.

Your primitive *old brain* reacts in *self-defense* when you feel you have been verbally attacked. Use the *merging technique* to delay counterattacking when blame is directed at you. This delay gives your *new brain* the time to reason and to focus on the communication by your partner. *Standing your ground* to resolve issues can be rewarding, if you use *soothing comments*, not acidic remarks. Through communication, marital bliss can become the norm. You and your spouse will then walk in a path of love.

— 13 —

Money Sense Matters

Henceforth I ask no good fortune,
I myself am good-fortune

—Walt Whitman

Money issues and misunderstandings are the number one reason why married couples fight and become estranged. Money problems can tear a couple apart and even lead them to the divorce court. In many marriage partnerships the husband and wife have an unwritten agreement on who will manage the budget, who will take care of bills and how any extra money will be spent. A general plan for money management is one of the keys to bliss in marriage, and agreement between two spouses on how to conduct that plan is part of the foundation for a long and happy marriage.

A crucial consideration in money management is the built-in attitudes each partner has upon entering the marriage. These attitudes were instilled a long time ago and set the stage for the way money will be viewed in the context of a relationship. For example, Jim grew up in an impoverished household. His parents divorced when he was nine years old, and his mother had to rely on his father's alimony. It took great effort on her part to get by on less. Whichever way she attempted to cut costs, she barely managed to pay the rent and buy food for herself and Jim. The scrimping and cutting back and having to get by with less, and sometimes none, gave Jim the fear of being poor. He had an aversion to apartment living and made sure to own his home at the age of twenty-five while the fear of being poor always lurked in the background. This great fear governed his entire life and affected his marriage with frequent arguments about money.

Attitudes about money can arise not only from past conditioning but also from present beliefs about what money represents. Money and monetary possessions have always made the world go around, in addition to love. Having money can mean many things to individuals. The first is freedom from poverty and scarcity, along with the uplifting feeling that all is possible with the means to experience better living conditions and to win at love. Money can also represent a settling of scores, a vindication after poor treatment by peers, relatives and societal attitudes toward the less fortunate.

Striking it rich in marriage has always been an unspoken wish of some individuals. For example, when a man dates the boss's daughter or woos the unattainable rich girl, he covets her as a material possession, which becomes the primary reason for the relationship. Separating money from love becomes an impossible task since the two overlap. These attitudes later undermine the marriage with unspoken regrets that one or both partners could have done better had they married into money or achieved greater riches within the marriage. A man can be proud of the beauty he sees in his intended bride, but this sense will be heightened if she also possesses wealth. For a woman the same attitude applies in that her husband's wealth will finally free her from hardships and having to make do with less, and will assure her financial future. Of course money matters. As the popular saying goes: "Poor or rich, it's good to have money." But when money is the primary goal in life, it distorts the real values that life has to offer such as unconditional love, affection, trust and friendship.

Carl Rogers, the humanistic psychologist, postulated that "the therapist experiences unconditional positive regard for the client" (Monte, 1991). Unconditional positive regard can also be translated into unconditional love. Unconditional love means loving your spouse even when he or she has made a mistake or unknowingly acted contrary to your wishes—for example, by spending a substantial amount of money on a purchase not previously agreed upon by both of you. That doesn't mean that you should overlook the large expenditure. All it means is that you need to voice your objection without criticism, sarcasm or reminders of past mistakes, and to trust your spouse with money even if an error in judgment has occurred.

What's Behind Excess Spending?

When does a spouse break rules and what are the motives behind it? Many times a spouse will make impulsive purchases without knowing why. The reasons can be numerous. Let's take a look at some of the most prevalent ones. The first and most important reason for making impulsive costly purchases without consulting the other spouse may be a desire to restore balance in the relationship. One spouse may want to regain some power lost to the other spouse.

It is also possible that the offending spouse, whether husband or wife, has ambivalent feelings about the relationship and is trying to fill a void that exists in the marriage. If the void is caused by a lack of attention, the spouse may be attempting to get attention by overspending.

Or the spouse may want to settle a score by getting back at the other spouse for humiliation, insults or an overwhelming sense of being controlled. These unfulfilled needs set in motion not only the overspending of precious financial resources, but also a downward spiral in a financial vicious cycle.

Another reason for money mismanagement is simply a lack of financial planning within the marriage. For example, a couple might have begun their life together by haphazardly letting each other overspend without objection, not setting precise rules on who would take care of the budget and how funds would be allocated. This lack of rules on money management becomes an ingrained habit that's hard to break, and as a result, the couple gets swallowed up in a "rob Peter to pay Paul" remedial system. Other problems can arise in arrangements where "his money" and "her money" are separate for each partner's sense of autonomy. This arrangement is workable as long as no one feels cheated or burdened with an unfair share of financial responsibility.

Money Management

What then are the rules for financial planning for a couple who desires more than anything to have peace and harmony when it comes to money? The first thing a couple needs to do is sit down and devise a budget, then stick to it no matter what comes along to disrupt it. In that budget all moneys will be pooled together, or divided into separate budgets. A budget worksheet is the first step in getting a bird's-eye view on where the money goes. A "Necessary Monthly Expenses" is the first budget to set up. It includes only necessary expenditures for each month. An example follows.

NECESSARY MONTHLY EXPENSES

(Sample for photocopying)

1. Food $_____

2. Housing $_____

3. Car Insurance $_____

4. Car Maintenance $_____

5. Utilities $_____

6. Medical Insurance $_____

7. Taxes $_____

8. School Expenses $_____

9. Retirement Savings $_____

10. Rainy-Day Savings $_____

TOTAL NECESSARY
EXPENSES $_____

INCOME $_____

NECESSARY EXPENSES
(SUBTRACT) $_____

REMAINDER $1,284 (example)_____

Next, set up a separate budget for your monthly discretionary expenses. Take the Remainder sum ($1,284 in the example above) to begin your discretionary budget.

DISCRETIONARY MONTHLY EXPENSES	
(Sample for photocopying)	
1. Clothing and Shoes	$_____
2. Entertainment	$_____
3. Vacation	$_____
4. Furniture	$_____
5. Other Expenses	$_____
REMAINDER	$1,284 (example)_____
DISCRETIONARY EXPENSES (SUBTRACT)	$_____
TOTAL (+OR-)	$_____

If your discretionary budget total is a minus (chances are it may be), then you will need to adjust those expenses accordingly by eliminating some or scaling them down. For example, if a piece of furniture will take a good chunk out of your budget, then you need to plan on reducing vacation or clothing expenditures. A discretionary budget will help you focus to see where your priorities are and what to cut down. Once you have your monthly necessary and discretional budget, you must stick to it.

Unforeseen events can set stumbling blocks in the relationship as well as in your budget. The loss of a job, a long illness not covered by insurance, or a change in careers can all strain a marriage to a point where the partners lose sight of their love for each other. If you've kept to your budget, you then dig into your rainy-day savings and sleep without fear of what tomorrow may bring. In good times some surplus in these rainy-day savings can be used for additional expenses. What is important is being prepared when disaster strikes. If one or both of you find yourselves suddenly without a job, you'll still have each other to lean on. You'll also have the security of knowing that you both agreed beforehand on a financial plan that will save you in the end. You can also seek professional advice through a financial consultant if you have a surplus and want to put your money to work doubly for you.

Usually when a couple makes sacrifices for a common goal, the hardships become minimal. As long as this goal is visible and focused upon, there is no way to lose sight of it. A helpful way to measure your financial status is to keep a "progress chart." Let's say, for example, that you want to save enough money for a luxury item such as a new car, an expensive piece of furniture, an entertainment center in your home, or maybe an addition to your house. That project or goal needs to be visually charted on a bulletin board or paper and mounted on the wall, so that you can "see" the progress you are making toward that goal. Use red stickpins to gauge your progress toward a car, for example, by drawing the outline of a car with an advancing line of stickpins as you save money toward your goal. This visual project is a strategy to encourage you to reach your goals.

A film that left an indelible mark upon me in relation to goal setting was *The Inn of The sixth Happiness*, based on Alan Burgess's novel *The Small Woman*. Ingrid Bergman plays Gladys Aylward, an English parlor maid whose goal is to reach China to become a missionary. Her goal is thwarted when the English mission tells her she is not qualified for the position. Determined in her calling, she then contacts a travel agency and pays a few shillings on account. Continuing to make payments over a period of months, she finally succeeds in meeting the enormous sum of forty-seven pounds, and ten shillings for her fare to China.

Such is the power of will, and it could be yours too. Small increments in saving and small steps in systematic cost-cutting of your expenses can lead to big investments for your future.

To cut down on entertainment expenses, for example, you can look for free family outings and low-cost entertainment. Most cities offer free or low-cost entertainment through museums, botanical gardens, libraries (lectures, books and videos), low-fee classes through the Parks and Recreation Department and extension schools, fairs where you can bring your own picnic foods, summer activities, swimming, and hobby clubs to name a few. Some of the best entertainment we have enjoyed as a couple and family were found through these avenues where we spent the least and enjoyed ourselves the most.

Living within your means is another cost-cutting living style. It does not mean depriving yourselves completely, but being selective in choosing the leisure and entertainment you desire most while skipping the things that matter least to you. Living within your means does not mean having to save every penny for day-to-day living. It only means skipping a few movies out on Saturday nights so that you can save for that special big event you don't want to miss. It means selectively choosing what is best for the two of you. By following a simple plan and sticking to it, you will have peace of mind and relief from the financial worries that undermine marriages. The benefits of following a reasonable and prudent financial course can save your relationship and your marriage.

Monitoring your financial progress can become a good habit that benefits your marital health and creates peace of mind. You can set up budget charts such as the ones shown earlier. A detailed listing of your entertainment spending can also help you see where your money goes. Charts for separate expense categories (food, clothing, etc.) can be extremely helpful when small expenditures add up to a considerable amount each month.

Last but not least, a separate credit-card register can reveal where your expenditures seem to disappear into a black hole each month, then suddenly reappear like a supernova when the monthly statement arrives. A good way to monitor your credit card expenses is to allocate a credit-card budget, and to deduct each purchase right away.

It is never too early to plan your financial security whether it is retirement, buying a home or large purchase, or investments for the future.

Exercise 21: Our Financial Goals

In your journal write down a list of financial goals you and your spouse can foresee for the future and how you will achieve those goals. Set a financial meeting time every now and then to monitor those goals, and keep a schedule of when those meetings are to take place. Condense your list of financial goals on an index card, in order of importance, with the most important goal at the top. Title that card "Our Financial Goals."

Conclusion

Money issues can become the number one cause of fighting, which can lead over time to serious problems in the marriage. Attitudes about money that are brought into the marriage can also contribute to strife and non-cooperation in the relationship. *Unconditional love* can lead to *unconditional trust* in money management. Look into the reasons why your spouse has overstepped your agreements on spending money. Are there legitimate reasons for these expenses, or is it in retribution for lack of love, attention or praise?

Set up budgets to give yourselves *peace of mind* and *financial security*. Use a credit-card check-register system to keep you in balance. Look into free or low-cost entertainment available in your city, at libraries, parks or gardens, or public events. *Live within your means* to meet your budget and ensure *savings for the future*.

— 14 —

External and Internal Forces in Marriage

---

*The degree of difficulty in resolving a problem
depends on your perspective of the situation.*

In the preface of this book we saw that the human
personality is as complex as the facets of a diamond. And
just as a polishing is in order when a diamond becomes
clouded or dull, a fresh outlook is in order when we have
lost our way in the maze of life.

Shortly after birth, there is a freshness in the way we
view the world around us, and as we grow up, with every
new experience we become attuned to various other new
experiences. We make great plans for ourselves and see our
future unbounded by our imagination. In time, though,
some of us lose sight of those plans, and we ask ourselves,
where have all the years gone?

A similar realization that all is not well often comes in
the early years of marriage with uneasy, unconscious
nagging feelings. These doubts can be instigated by both
internal and external forces that bear upon a married couple,
undermining all their efforts to live blissful lives. What are
these concealed internal and external forces, and how do
they affect the marriage institution? Besides upbringing,

those forces include the family legacy, society's influence and peer pressure, predatory human beings encroaching on the marriage, and the social conditioning operating at the subconscious level of the mind. We will examine these forces in detail in this chapter. By becoming more aware of these forces, we can build a strong marriage foundation and preserve the marriage institution.

Why Marriage Evolved

The marriage institution, in existence now for approximately three to four thousand years, has evolved to protect two individuals from obstacles and destructive powers. Among the benefits and advantages of marriage, the most compelling is the preservation and perpetuation of the human race as well as of the individuals themselves. This benefit speaks to each married member to honor the wedding contract and protect it from harm: "to have and to hold, to forsake all others, to cherish and love, in sickness and in health."

There are other valid reasons for protecting marriage in addition to the ones mentioned above. In ancient times, marriage was a contract between clans and families of clans. The bond gave further protection to women from predatory men who would rape them or do away with their children. These wandering unattached men on the prowl would secure for themselves a woman to continue their direct line of progeny, and keep their family's riches (even though those "riches" may have been only a corner in a cave or a thatched hut where their belongings were protected by those grown children). These children in turn would have their safety assured when they bonded with a partner at maturity age. Nowadays the picture has changed, with grown children soon going into the world to make their own way and find their own nests, leaving their parents to fend for themselves for their safety and livelihood. These days, some of us are fortunate enough to have what we call financial safeguards such as IRAs, life insurance, and 401(k) plans to assure our future golden years. For others, the grown children become their sole support.

In the days of agricultural settlements, the father and mother, and the children too, pitched in to help around the farm or garden plot. As the agrarian society gave way to the factory and foundry age, the father left the home to travel to the cities. It was about that time that the absent father loomed in every child's life. The child would then become the protector of the family at the age of ten or younger. The young adolescent ceased being a child and became a young adult by necessity. Ill prepared for that role, the child repressed his or her own childhood, and perhaps felt the longing forevermore.

Now think of a present-day child, ten or fifteen years of age, having to become a parent to his or her parents in a case where the father may be emotionally distant from the mother, or where either parent is suffering from some form of addiction: alcohol, drugs, gambling, or sex. Besides having to mature suddenly, that child now has to cope with the father's or mother's illness. In the child's brain, the imprint of an ailing family becomes the blueprint for his or her own family in the future. Along with becoming highly stressed, that child will suffer lifelong effects by repeating this cycle of illness again and again.

In the early phases of some civilizations, the procreation of the human masses was often incestuous. Even in ancient myths, the deities of Roman times married each other. One example is the incest of the ancient Egyptian pharaohs; a brother would marry a sister to continue the same dynasty. And even in our times, rape and incest are committed by individuals to further their own pathological thoughts of power and the fantasy of perpetual youth. These ancient, misguided cultural traditions contributed to genetic deviations that ended those same dynasties.

In our present-day culture there are similar destructive forces at work, aimed at undermining the marriage tradition. Some of these destructive forces, such as family legacy, were in place before the marriage partners were born, while others were instated, perpetuated, or abetted by the spouses themselves.

Family Legacy

Before a child is born, many factors go into the equation that will decide the fate of that child and what course his or her life will take. These factors are the internal forces at work through the family lineage. The first internal force is the blueprinting the parents acquired as infants themselves from their own parents. These blueprints, or patterns of attitudes and behavior, can often be traced back several generations in the genealogical tree. Any aberration or deviation from the path of "normalcy" — defined as a close-knit family that protects the child in every way, both physically and emotionally — will have a direct bearing upon a child born several generations in the future. Such aberrations could range anywhere from patterns of despondency to violent or addictive behavior, or failure to achieve happiness in life.

Besides those genealogical legacies, parental role-modeling will also influence the life of that child born generations down the line. These patterns, with slight behavior deviations, can undo the chances of a child for a happy and blissful life. As that child grows up with his or her interpretation of life, this legacy pattern becomes compounded by the impulse to survive at all cost. Therefore the internal forces of genealogy, blueprinting and role-modeling will all come into play in the game of survival.

Society's Influence

While internal forces are at work to undermine an individual's life balance, external forces also weigh heavily in that balance. What are those external disrupters, and where do they originate? To begin with, let's look at society at large and the subliminal cues and messages it directs at the average male and female beginning in childhood and continuing through adulthood. Every one of us has experienced, every day of our lives, the messages and reminders thrown at us from all directions of society. These messages arrive through the media, television, billboards, movies, magazines or just plain word of mouth.

How can "innocent" messages affect our lives to the point of changing our behavior and future? It is very simple; it is done through the subliminal, subconscious conditioning of our thoughts. You might say, "Well, I have a mind of my own, and only I can decide whether something written or spoken will change my outlook on life." While we may have a mind of our own, our brain gets bombarded daily with subtle messages until those get programmed into our psyche to plague us later on.

Take, for example, peer pressure and how it affects our outlook on life. Among men and women, it is an accepted cultural attitude that sex is not only good for one's health of body and mind but can also be used as a vehicle for jokes and laughter. Therefore, sex jokes roll on in the workplace, in locker rooms, and at social gatherings. These jokes may make one chuckle and help pass the time, and that's harmless in itself. It's not that we can't laugh at our own foibles when it comes to sex, but that sex jokes are often used to condone unacceptable behavior. Repeating jokes about casual sex becomes a gratifying pastime that makes one feel good, or better, about one's own sexuality and casual sex. And any good feeling that seems to justify casual sex becomes fodder for conditioning the mind with permissive attitudes.

When a married man, for example, confides to another man that he has had a sexual encounter or an affair, the listener will usually smile casually and not pass judgment upon the speaker. A wink and a smile say it all: "You stud, how can you be so lucky?" Married men talk about their sexual conquests to impress other men, but more so to convince themselves that they are young and virile. Married women confide their infidelities to win approval from their like-minded peers and to reassure themselves that they are still attractive and lovable.

While both men and women who indulge in those errant paths find a temporary high in the delusion that they are loved, the time and energy they have used up has undermined their life goals. Infidelity tears down two stones for every stone that has built their life. It sets them back months or years in the pursuit of happiness.

Commercialism in today's society has not helped much, either, to alleviate the woes of married life or to help forge lasting relationships. It is estimated that billions of dollars are spent each year by consumers to trim down, beautify and attire themselves to please the other sex. Being health conscious is an advantage for a long and vital life, but obsessing with weight and looks is not. Each day, thousands of anorexic girls mount the treadmills of America and lose another pound from their already fragile body frame. This drain on the body eventually takes its toll and becomes irreversible.

Every day of every year our brain gets bombarded with images created by others. Even though we have a mind of our own, we cannot help absorbing those images into our psyche where they become permanently embedded. Those images can then become the blueprint for how we should look, dress, speak, and love.

Most of us have, at one time in our lives, thumbed through the pages of *Playboy* magazine or the like out of curiosity. The images in those pages were created to appeal to a titillating way of life. If *Playboy* and similar magazines had never come on the scene, would we have the notion that well-endowed women are more desirable? That notion need not have a strong influence on our minds unless we let it happen. Meanwhile, hundreds of thousands of women have undergone breast implants to look more like the so-called physically ideal woman. Today the fashion world is telling us that the slim woman without the big breasts is in. What will fashion tell us tomorrow? Furthermore, what will be the emotional effect on all the women who have had a surgeon cut into their breasts to implant these foreign objects? Will these women go rushing back to have them cut out? Again, much energy, as well as money, was wasted to please an ephemeral fad that one hundred years from now is sure to be looked upon with curiosity.

We have all waited at the check out stand and seen the array of magazines displayed there. The gamut runs from how to make a lover scream in sexual ecstasy, to cooking the best summer meals, dishing the latest gossip on celebrities, divining the future through your horoscope, creating the perfect house and being the perfect housewife, to magazines for men only, as a pipeline of mass merchandising for

imprinting and role-modeling. All these meteoric trajec-
tories in formula-based advice are followed religiously by
the masses.

Through the images in these magazines we have come to
associate certain looks with sex and beauty, and our brain
encodes these new limits and rejects other looks and other
possible realities. We expend much energy to impress,
cajole, astonish and seduce our mates by imitating these
images so that we can gain love. It's not that any of these
suggested methods of pleasing our mates is unacceptable.
The only thing wrong with this approach is that we have
used precious energies to build ephemeral worlds for
ourselves and rejected other realms that are valid in
themselves.

Take, for example, the analogy in one *Star Trek* episode
where the planet's inhabitants had one half of their face
black and the other half white. Two of the inhabitants were
fighting each other to the death, and a spectator, a visitor
from another planet, asked why they hated and fought each
other, considering that they were both identical. "Can't you
see?" said one of them. "I am black on the right side, and he's
black on the left side." This analogy can be applied to any
physical looks: There are tall people and short people and
some in between; there are slim and heavyset people; there
are all types of facial contours and colors of skin, hair and
eyes; and still we are the same. Who is to say which is better?
The distinctions might never have been made unless
someone could profit from it by brainwashing people to
believe that one type was better than another.

If we closely examined these questions as a neutral third
party having landed from another planet, we would be
confounded and puzzled as to why one type of feature
should be better than another. Apparently we as a society

have allowed these physical features to be judged according to standards set by others.

But we could also have set up a different model of attributes to be valued: for example, people who feel each other's pain and joys as if they were their own, people who value each other for who they are and not what they can bring, or men and women who stabilize each other's moods and behaviors as in a homeostatic seesaw. These men and women, who would zoom inside another's psyche and read their thoughts, would overlook the outer physical shell of a human being to reach the precious soul. If we carefully looked within, we would find that our real being is very much like these super beings. We are beings who seek love, and each one of us has that precious capacity to love from the time we are born.

Predators

Predatory human beings are another force that tears at the marriage fabric to undermine its benefits and reasons for being. The search for love can be a lifetime quest for anyone. We become vulnerable through love and validated by love while perpetuating this life on earth. We all know that men and women do not live by bread alone. We seek a mate for companionship, warmth and growth, but above all we search for another to authenticate that we are not alone in this life. Unfortunately, the search for a mate is sometimes pursued without discrimination, when seeking love at any cost. This quest can then involve chipping away at other people's marriages. We all know how this stealing from another is conducted: The "other" man or woman covets a married individual and takes her or him away by cajoling, feeding their ego, and tapping into the suggestive attitudes projected by the media and society. This snatching of another's spouse is done by taking advantage of their vulnerability.

Consider, for example, a spouse who is unhappy in a marriage. This unhappiness may have been brought about by one or the other spouse, or both, through alienation, abuse, plain numbness of feelings, or simply a lack of understanding what a marriage relationship entails. The unhappy spouse will eventually turn to another outside the marriage to satisfy unfulfilled needs, even though he or she may know the consequences. The energy that spouse expends outside the marriage would be better used within the marriage. We may think that extramarital love is more exciting and challenging, but marital love achieves higher feelings similar to a supernatural state of being.

Benefits of Love Within the Marriage

Love within the marriage becomes the reason for living and a lifetime goal. When two people are in love, they experience a state of being unlike any other. They become attuned to each other's needs and desires, and complement each other's life. Take, for example, a satisfied and happy married couple. They would have mastered communication with each other, respected and supported each other's challenging needs for growth and wishes in life, and enjoyed their mutual proximity and presence. This homeostatic relationship contributes to an overall state of natural well-being. With a harmonious state of mind come natural energies that contribute not only to a couple's permanent state of bliss but also to a life that is creative in all other endeavors.

In Chapter 10 we saw how the psychologist Abraham Maslow scaled his hierarchy of needs that must be met before self-actualization can be achieved. First we must have our basic physiological needs met, then our needs for safety and security. In a healthy and loving marriage relationship, you would also have reached the third rung of that scale, belongingness and love, and be on your way to meeting your esteem needs, the mastery of skills that you were meant to have, and ultimately achieving self-actualization, the highest and best self that you can possibly be. While each individual works on their own toward that end, two individuals in a loving relationship can achieve those goals faster and create a life full of riches. Those riches will include not only love, but the knowledge and wisdom that will bring rewards in material riches and ensure economic security.

Exercise 22: Enhancing Our Future

This exercise will build on Exercise 10 in Chapter 7. Go to your genealogical chart and observe the direction your ancestors took in life. You may have had illustrious ancestors who were successful in their careers and life goals. You may also have had ancestors who experienced the downfalls that can occur in malfunctioning families where an oppressive atmosphere prevents growth. Think about the course of events their lives took and how it affected your generation.

Now turn to your journal and write down how you want your own future married life to progress. What can you do to influence the course of your life so that progress becomes as natural as breathing air? On the next page you will find an example of setting up a course of events to influence your future in a progressive way. Transfer the highlights of your goals to an index card and title this card "Enhancing Our Future Married Life."

Steps for Enhancing Our Future

1. Establish a loving and respectful relationship with my wife/husband.

2. See to our children's needs and safe future.

3. Draw up a plan for future financial stability.

4. Set up a timetable for each goal.

5. Reward ourselves for each successful goal accomplished.

6. Spread the word around to family and friends about the commitment we have to our marriage and the respect we have for each other and how it has helped us achieve marital bliss.

To help enhance your future and keep your marriage going in the right direction, you should review your index cards once a month, or as often as you can. Remember that practice is what will change undermining behavior and firmly establish the desirable attributes you now possess. Above all, remember that merging with your spouse is not only necessary but imperative to wholesome mental health and progressive attitudes.

Conclusion

We are subjected to various external and internal powerful forces that can undermine our chances for happiness. An absent father, patterns of addiction in the family tree, alienation and role-modeling are the internal obstacles. External forces such as subliminal messages fed into our consciousness by commercialism can lead us to unconditionally follow their every cue in their quest for profit. These cues can give you a false sense of who you should be, how you should look and what you should like.

The sexual attitudes of commercialism may also breach your psyche to become part of your conditioning. Predatory human beings may invade your marital life and put obstacles in the path to your own happiness.

Love within the *marriage* is an experience unlike any other. *A couple in love* can live in total harmony and can face obstacles to their marriage with common determination. *Enhancing your future* is your *life's vision,* and *living in love* is your *life's purpose.*

Part III

THE BUTTERFLY

— 15 —

Sexual Love

I draw you close to me, you woman,
I cannot let you go, I would do you good,
I am for you, and you are for me, not only for our own sake,
but for others' sakes,
Envelop'd in you sleep greater heroes and bards,
They refuse to awake at the touch of any man but me.

—Walt Whitman

Sexual love. We long for it, we imagine it and we seek it. Our bodies, minds and souls prepare for it as generations before us have prepared themselves through mating rituals. Sexual love envelops us in its warm embrace while giving meaning to our existence as a couple and the blending of souls in that physical union. Sex and sexual love can be mystifying and driven by hidden motivations in our life, such as our need for validation, admiration and feeling loved.

Sex between a man and a woman becomes an all-encompassing emotion when fulfilled through mutual love and affection. Both partners then know that their emotional trust is secure with each other. But sex is also influenced by factors outside of the marriage: by role-modeling, and their idea of what sex should be.

Sex Education in Adolescence

During puberty, sex becomes a driving emotion that overwhelms and mystifies the young adult. At about age fourteen the adolescent male develops facial and pubic hair, and typically begins to discover girls and feel drawn to them. At a slightly earlier age of twelve or thirteen, a girl starts menstruating and develops breasts, which give her proud but baffling emotions with feelings of self-consciousness about the effect it has on boys. In the next three to four years, these young adults go through great confusion and tension regarding their bodies. The temptations are then great to become sexually active and uncover this mystery called sex that they hear and see all around them.

Unfortunately the confusion between sex and love occurs at the age when a young male or female often has no guidelines other than those taught by sex education in the schools or through the surreptitious magazine viewing of nudity and pornography. It's not that sex education in the schools isn't worthwhile and enlightening. It's just that it takes a clinical approach that separates sex from love and sets that tone for an individual's future sex life. Schools do not have the capacity to teach love in the arena of sex, nor can they prevent the imprinting and negative role-modeling that the world-at-large projects.

At home, there are often taboos and a lack of parental education, as well as the absence of affection between the parents. This all contributes to the adolescent's confusion, and erroneous opinions of what sex is. The lack of parental communication about sex is another area that stunts maturing youth, who are left with a negative street vocabulary and insulting sex terms. The young adult is then forced to incorporate in his or her psyche what remains in the periphery: only what they see and hear about sex in the media and from their peers.

Seeing affectionate love between parents when they kiss and hug can be a positive force in a maturing young adult. This role-modeling will be perceived in the impressionable young mind as showing that sex and love are inseparable. On the other hand, if sex in the home was marred by repeated negative experiences or trauma, sex and love will be sharply separated in the adolescent's mind.

Sexual Love in Marriage

Sexual love or making love means not only fulfilling an urge or finding pleasure for yourself but also pleasing someone else in the union of two bodies. Giving that pleasure to your mate becomes the most satisfying aspect in lovemaking, and the feeling of accomplishment in having pleased the other through your love is highly rewarding. Sexual love will bathe you with its glow in the aftermath, and give you an aura of pleasurable thoughts about your partner while keeping the sexual flame alive indefinitely.

Now, if sex is focused in only one direction—that is, satisfying only oneself—then sex remains just sex and its aftermath is of short duration. This kind of sex merely reassures us that we are sexual beings without bestowing the benefits of a mingling of minds and souls.

Similarly, if an individual is driven to sex as a conquest, a tally or a scoring, sex will be unfulfilling and that individual will keep searching for something that remains a mystery and will keep trying to fill an infinite void. It is difficult, to say the least, to find fulfillment in sex when that person, whether young or mature, cannot fathom what they are searching for. It would be like looking for a needle in a haystack or going on an undefinable pursuit.

This type of sex is usually conducted in brief encounters, one-night stands, affairs, or even in a loveless marriage with mechanical gestures. In that case the marriage stagnates as a phantom union and can become the repository for ills and unhappiness. Usually this unhappiness results from mis-understandings by one partner or both, or from unresolved conflicts and issues being continuously swept under the rug. The avoidance of issues is also the avoidance of having to face truths, and the fear of all the accumulated anger toward one another. This suppressed rage cannot be contained forever. Eventually sexual love is gone from the marriage, and only sex remains to lull oneself to sleep.

Extramarital Sex

In extramarital sex, the errant spouse has breached the marriage commitment. Many problems can occur in a relationship to lead a partner into breaching the bounds of the marriage. They include poor communication, un-satisfied needs, lack of affection, lack of praise and recognition, or a punishing spouse. Another reason could simply be refusing to grow old or mature within the marriage relationship. Sometimes a birth in the family creates stress with the additional duties in a marriage, or a traumatic event can drive one or the other spouse to seek outside sexual interest.

In many instances, one or the other spouse has for some time contemplated a way out of the marriage, but could not bring themselves to initiate this move. Therefore having the affair and leaving telltale signs for the other spouse to discover precipitates divorce. Unsettled scores between two spouses may lead one spouse to take revenge upon the other. A spouse with low self-esteem may even sub-consciously allow their partner to stray outside the marriage in the erroneous belief that others can satisfy their partner more.

Sexual Love

To better understand sexual love it is necessary to break it down into its two components: sex and love. Over the years, many research surveys have been done on attitudes and behavior regarding sex and love (Leigh, 1989; Quadagno & Sprague, 1991). The results vary widely. At one end of the spectrum, couples reported that they engage in sex without the love component, while the majority of couples said that love and sex could not exist one without the other in their relationship. At the other end of the spectrum, couples in long married relationships claimed that love could exist without sex. These older couples contented themselves only with platonic feelings of security and affection (Carroll et al., 1985; Clark & Hatfield, 1989). Nevertheless, love and sexual attraction and intimacy remain closely interrelated for most couples.

In other studies, men found it easier than women to have sex for only physical release with no emotional attachment (Carroll et al., 1985; Clark & Hatfield, 1989; Randolf & Winstead, 1988). Women, on the other hand, could not enjoy sexual intercourse without a love commitment. More recently, studies have consistently shown that men's attitudes toward sex without love have changed, and that 81 percent of men and 91 percent of women now say that sexual intercourse is closely interrelated with affection (Kallen & Stephenson, 1982). In the age of AIDS and other sexually transmitted diseases, monogamy is also on the increase, and that has given time for those relationships to take root and blossom into intimacy and long-term commitments.

In the case of sexually infatuated love, the one who is in "love" sees the object of his or her affection as inspiring the most desirous, romantic, physiologically intense period of their life. This time of intense infatuation can include extreme anxiety as well as euphoric feelings, periods of riding high with anticipation and then crashing down with extreme disappointment. Such exciting but short-lived entanglement only brings loss in the end. Infatuated love is built upon the premise that suddenly the world around the lovers has become a magical place. All commitments and realities are swept aside. Sometimes the lovers cannot see any imperfections in one another, and each accepts the other as flawless (Crooks & Baur, 1993).

After this intense "love" affair dwindles and dies, the participants ask themselves what in the world were they thinking and how could they have been so blind? These wild and unrealistic expectations of another are born out of unfulfilled needs that the participants bring into the relationship, such as extreme hunger for love, self-doubts about their sexuality, or past traumas. These expectations are, again, built on the desire that this "lover" will make things right for them once and for all.

On the other hand, sexual love, affection, commitment and a solid grounding in reality are the seeds that sprout and grow strong into a loving and long-lasting relationship. These, of course, take time to develop and the partners must come to accept the flaws in each other as well as the desired qualities. Each one knows that these surmountable flaws will not detract from the respect and love commitment they have for each other.

Sexual Dysfunctions

Sexual love can also be hindered by physical or hidden ailments. A lack of knowledge concerning one's sexual body and its capacity for love can also keep an adult from experiencing sexual love. Other hindrances can be past rage, a settling of scores for wrongdoing, and lack of communication. Physical ailments such as prostate infections or cancer, breast cancer, recurring vaginal infections, debilitating or sexually transmitted disease, diabetes, heart condition, anemia and lack of stamina can all affect sexual love. Lack of enthusiasm for life, low sexual desire or plain boredom can also be a turnoff to lovemaking. These factors can influence the sexual life of a couple and test their patience and perseverance in the realm of sexual love.

Physical sexual dysfunctions within the marriage can take many forms. The first one that slows down lovemaking to a halt is impotence in the male or anorgasmia in the female. The term *impotence* comes from the Latin word meaning "without power." The term's negative connotations of lacking power when it comes to making love can add to a man's distress. A better term is *erectile dysfunction* or *erectile inhibition* (Levine & Althof, 1991). These erectile inhibitions can begin at a young age or develop in later years. They can also be lifelong or, more commonly, temporary.

Many factors can cause the erectile inhibition, including exhaustion from stress or overwork, poor blood flow to the penis or pressure caused by prostate problems. It is estimated that prostate problems will occur in about 5 percent of men by the age of forty, and in 15 to 25 percent by age sixty-five. Most men wait too long to have prostate examinations out of denial of any difficulties. What is important for a man is to be aware of the possibility of prostate problems and not to ignore it. A man's ability to have a healthy sexual life can add more enjoyment to his married life.

Anorgasmia is the preferred term for female inhibited orgasm, rather than the term *frigidity*, which has negative and inaccurate connotations of an unloving spouse. Anorgasmia, the inability to experience orgasm, can be a lifelong inhibition or a temporary one. A woman with this condition does not experience arousal that eventually leads to orgasm.

Women have been led to believe that if they cannot have an orgasm without masturbating, then something is wrong with them. Nothing can be farther from the truth. Masturbation with or without male penetration can be satisfying to a woman and her partner. Communicating to her partner how she would like to experience orgasm can also be helpful if the partner genuinely takes an active role in pleasing her.

Erectile inhibition and anorgasmia are both treatable and should not create major disturbances in a marriage. There are many clinics and sex therapists who can help a couple to resolve their sexual difficulties. A member of the clergy, a rabbi or a priest can also help a couple through counseling or referrals.

A couple deeply committed to each other will endure these setbacks and rebound back to normal intimacy and sexual love. Transcending difficulties presents not only a challenge to a couple but also a renewed sense in their marriage that despite all odds they will stay together and reap the rewards later on.

This brings to mind the poem "Still Here" by Langston Hughes:

> *I've been scarred and battered.*
> *My hopes the wind done scattered.*
> *Snow has friz me, sun has baked me.*

Looks like between 'em
They done tried to make me
Stop laughin', stop lovin', stop livin' —
But I don't care!
I'm still here!

This same unvanquished feeling can be fueled in the marriage not only by the commitment the partners have for each other, but by the conviction that the institution of marriage is sacred and important to all their aspirations in life together.

Nurturing Sexual Love

A thorough knowledge of the sexual anatomy of both men and women is advantageous in satisfying a partner's requests in lovemaking. There are many excellent sex manuals and textbooks describing the human body that can enhance pleasure in a couple's lovemaking. This chapter will not go into details regarding human anatomy, but an explanation of the sexual and emotional commitment between marital partners is in order.

Before the sexual revolution of the sixties, sexual love was considered appropriate for serving purely romantic purposes only until the end of the honeymoon, and then its purpose was to have children. The current trend of thought regarding sexual love is that a thriving sexual relationship with a spouse contributes to the well-being of both partners. Sexual love can be defined as the fulfillment of both spouses in being gratified, validated and trusted, through giving themselves to please the other and merging their bodies sexually to experience ecstasy. The release of tension in reaching orgasm not only completes both man and woman but also reassures them that their partner is the right partner, the one who is most satisfying, and the one who is respected, loved and cherished.

Dysfunction in achieving sexual love can grind lovemaking to a halt. As we discussed earlier, the factors contributing to those dysfunctions include low sexual desire, erroneous perceptions of what constitutes "great lovemaking," and repressed conflicts. These roadblocks to a relationship can lead to great unhappiness and divorce. To begin with, there is no standard for what makes the best lovemaking between a couple. This is defined by the couple themselves and their preferences in lovemaking. For example, the super and multiple orgasms touted in litera-ture and in popular magazines can be the source of much unhappiness when a couple feels that their lovemaking is below standard. The comparison is unwarranted because every individual and every couple has different perceptions of what they like. Furthermore, there are also different preferences on exactly where and how a partner likes to be touched or fondled for the utmost in pleasure—this varies from individual to individual. Therefore, a standard set by these so-called sex authorities can be misleading and completely erroneous. No two sexual experiences are the same between two partners, let alone from couple to couple. Sexual love between two spouses is unique and comparable to no other.

A stable and loving relationship that includes sexual love cements the marriage and enhances the likelihood that the marriage will continue throughout the couple's lives. In addition, the children born in that marriage will have the stability and security that comes from witnessing love and affection between their parents. These children will also grow to fulfill their promise in life by being free of an unhappy parental legacy. A child growing up in a restrained and miserable atmosphere in the home will feel unhappy that his or her presence was not sufficient to make the parents happy. That child will come to one conclusion: that he or she is not lovable. Therefore, this child will carry lifelong scars of feeling unloved.

Although low sexual desire can stem from a variety of internal causes such as depression or lack of joy in one's life, external factors can also contribute. The day-to-day routine of making love in the same fashion and same place, for example, can cause boredom over a period of months and years.

Making love to one's spouse should become an occasion for creativity. Places and rituals can vary beyond the bedroom. Imaginative and erotic lovemaking can occur in the living room, surrounded by candles or on a rug in front of the fireplace; in the bathtub, after maximum relaxation; in the shower; in a secluded countryside spot; below the stars in your backyard (if you have complete privacy, of course); in the afternoon, at unexpected times (while children are at school); and in many various combinations of sexual positions agreeable to both partners. If these possibilities do not work to create exciting lovemaking, then a medical examination is necessary to exclude physical problems.

If one of the partners still persists with low sexual desire, then there could be another cause such as resentment toward the other for some past wrongs or unresolved issues. Unresolved conflicts can be the source of many sexual dysfunctions. These conflicts include past or present unsettled disagreements, low or no respect for a spouse, erroneous thoughts about how a spouse should look or behave in lovemaking, and disagreements regarding finances or childrearing. Lack of love in the family of origin, social conditioning, misinformation from the external world, and sexual stereotypes can also contribute.

Both men and woman can fall prey to fanciful thoughts fueled daily by glossy images of sexuality portrayed in the media. The beauty standards of movies, magazines and the fashion industry convey the idea that external beauty and sexual love are the same. But nothing can be farther from the truth. For example, beauty queens and supermodels can very distant emotionally and even nonsexual. The grueling routine in the fashion world and the constant exposure to cameras and the public eye can become a turnoff for some of them.

Sexual love does not consist of the physical dimension only. There is also the internal dimension of sexual love that includes love and respect for one another, admiration, skills in lovemaking, a desire to please the other and a shared history. When both spouses experience sexual love with each other, the excitement and passion revealed in their bodies fuel the marriage and bring bliss. They can gaze into each other's eyes and find in those depths their own love reflected and the desire to be one with their spouse.

Briefly, that is the essence of sexual love in marriage — loving with one's whole body, mind and soul. It is the inner qualities, the essence of their spouse, that the other spouse desires more than anything in the world.

Communicating about Sex

Communicating your sexual preferences to your spouse can be invigorating to the sexual love life in your marriage. Begin gradually, indicating by touch at first, then verbally as communications flow from one spouse to the other. There are many types of tactile preferences when it comes to sexual love, and verbalizing them can be extremely gratifying. If one spouse is reluctant to discuss lovemaking, try at another relaxed time: perhaps while on an outing, while having a snack or meal or while holding each other close.

The requesting partner can say gently, for example: "I like it very much when you use light pressure. It gives me more pleasure." That can be taken as a request for additional touching, and not so much as criticism. You can express your feelings about sexual love with praise and with open-ended questions: "I really enjoyed how you ended our lovemaking, and next time I'd like to try lengthening our foreplay. How does that sound to you?" If your partner is reluctant to verbalize sexual matters, a question beginning with praise can put him or her at ease and encourage a reply. As always, try to find the right time to ask these questions, but not immediately after lovemaking. While your partner is basking in the afterglow, being asked to improve his or her performance next time can be a real letdown.

Empathy, and being interested in finding out and discussing your partner's needs, can also be most gratifying. Giving pleasure to your partner and listening to his or her specific requests can make your partner feel grateful and eager to want to reciprocate that lovemaking back to you. Listening actively will let your partner shed any fear about revealing their most intimate desires in lovemaking.

Example of Communicating after Lovemaking

He: What did you like most about our lovemaking tonight?

She: I liked your light touch and I especially enjoyed how you held me close.

He: I also enjoyed holding you close. I could feel your body being part of mine.

Example of Communicating after Lovemaking

She: I got a tremendous feeling from hearing you reach orgasm.

He: (laughing) I hope I wasn't too loud?

She: (stroking his back) The louder the better!

Many times we shy away from asking for specific touches or acts for fear of injuring our partner's pride. The way to avoid that is to start with praise and then finish with the request.

Exercise 23: Our Ideal Sexual Lovemaking

Turn now to your journal and list your desires, wishes and ideas for new ways to experience and improve sexual love with your spouse. If these are your wishes, then you need to initiate them and suggest them in a non-aggressive way, and at an appropriate time and place. Write down how and when you will go about executing this plan. It is preferable to use a *specific time and date* to carry out this plan. For example, if this is Monday, plan to carry out your next lovemaking in the manner you desire by next weekend or sooner. We all have the tendency to procrastinate and delay taking action of any kind when it demands a little effort on our part, or we may forget our good intentions altogether in the midst of a busy and active life.

Now transfer the highlights of your plan for improved lovemaking to an index card and title it "Our Ideal Sexual Lovemaking."

Conclusion

The physical union and blending of souls is experienced most profoundly in *sexual love*. To reach this pinnacle of human emotions we *value, cherish* and *respect* our spouses and verbalize our appreciation of their qualities through *praise* and *admiration*. *Sexual love* within the marriage and within a *committed relationship* surpasses any other sexual experience from past times and places. *Emotional commitment* to a spouse, without fear of betrayal, enhances the marriage and establishes more *trust*. *Sexual love* means pleasing yourself as well as your partner. Your sexual lovemaking experience is like no other, nor can it all be found in sex manuals or conveyed by sex authorities. The knowledge that you find in sexual literature can only enhance what is already within—your capacity to love sexually and unconditionally. Displays of *affection* within the marriage will convey to children that their parents love each other, and the children in turn will have a healthier, more mature attitude toward sexual love in their adult years.

16

The Harmonious Golden Years

Afoot and light-hearted I take to the open road,
healthy, free, the world before me,
The long brown path before me leading wherever I
choose.

—Walt Whitman

This is the beginning of a golden age for you and your spouse. Not a golden age in years, mind you, but in freedom of mind and spirit. The two of you are now standing at the threshold of great opportunities in new experiences, new sensations and new heights in your life. This would not have been possible if the two of you had not resolved to move on to a better relationship and breathe in the precious scents of life. This then is a time for the two of you to savor bliss in your marriage, to congratulate yourselves for getting there and to look at all the alternatives awaiting you as you reach peaks of contentment in a well-lived life.

A New Future

How you got there is only half the question, and by now, hopefully you have the answer. The other half is where do you go from here? Anytime in life is a good time to arrive at a point where you are free of worries and anxieties, the eternal questioning about your place in the scheme of things, and that all-consuming question, am I loved? You have conquered love because you were willing to open up wounds, dig into your past and make peace with the unsolved riddles of your life. By now you have kissed good-bye to all the unrealistic regrets that were standing in the way of your search for love. You have taken a good look in the mirror of life and have seen through the mists to where the real goal had lain in waiting: the attainment of your partner's love. Once you found that love nothing else seemed to matter: money, success, pride and envy. These were only plateaus that you, erroneously thought, had to climb to find this love.

To have earned love is an immense achievement. You may, after having found love, feel the pangs of regret that it did not happen sooner. It is not for us to know how fate guided our lives. We had no control over our previous generations, no control over how our parents lived their lives, and no control over our childhood. We do, however, have control from this point on over the next half of our lives.

Use my method of "Forward and Backward" if regrets still nag you from time to time. Whenever I indulge in bittersweet memories of my lost youth, young adulthood, motherhood, or a whole slew of "why this happened and why that happened," I project myself ten years into the future and see myself older with bitter and bigger regrets. I then rewind the film of my life and come back again to the present, feeling tremendously relieved to discover that I have not lost those ten years reminiscing about my lost past. I then say to myself: I still have ten more years ahead of me to undo and correct certain behaviors and patterns of thought that slow me down and use those energies in more constructive ways.

What we have now is the power to understand the past: how events in our parents' lives directly undermined our chances for happiness. The key is to come to terms with that knowledge. It is most rewarding to understand how events that influenced our parents' lives and personalities in turn governed our entire life's personality and behavior. What you have right now is the alternative and progressive life that should have been yours from the beginning. It is high time for you to claim it. What are these alternatives and how should you go about collecting those rewards? The answer is to visualize and project into the future the kind of lifestyle you aspire to have.

Your Health First

The first consideration for your future life is how your health will influence the steps this life will take. Without good health you may become limited in your endeavors. If you have serious health problems, now is the time to take care of them. Good health is the most precious commodity we have, and without this necessary component we may be slowed down on the road to self-actualization. Not that we cannot live lives of quiet determination and acceptance of certain permanent health problems. There are many who have reconciled themselves to deteriorating health and made the most of the precious years they have left. If, however, we have this opportunity to increase our health vitality, now is the time to begin.

Now that you are free of the stresses that you may have brought upon yourself through lack of knowledge, and free of the external stresses that undermined your outlook on life, you can take stock of your health. How are you going to tackle and rectify a lifetime of poor health decisions? First you need to see yourself as a healthy and vibrant individual. Once you have that image, you can then go about achieving it. Below you will find an example of health commitments you can follow:

Commitments to My Health

1. I will follow and stick to a program of physical exercise as well as a yearly medical checkup.

2. I will also see that my spouse gets a yearly medical checkup.

3. I will learn and follow healthy eating habits and help my spouse do the same.

4. I will erase from my mind physical beauty standards set by others and delight in who I am.

5. I will delight in my spouse's appearance and stop making comparisons.

6. My health is one of my life goals.

While these are worthwhile health endeavors to pursue, you must tackle them gradually. Health is an important component of a good life, but it should not take priority over all other aspects of life. We as a species have a tendency to be enthusiastic in our endeavors and goals, and sometimes we go overboard and become obsessive. For example, exercise can be a source of good health, but it can also become an obsessive-compulsive activity in which you sink all of your time and resources. Obsessive-compulsive behavior is usually done unconsciously to repress unacceptable thoughts or impulses, or to fill a deep void in one's life. By now, I hope you have filled these voids with love, companionship and wisdom. Nevertheless, the brain can still become susceptible to unconscious conditioning even when there is no void left to be filled.

Facing an Empty Nest

If you have raised children and gone through the joys, worries and stress involved in bringing them up, you may suddenly be faced with the "empty nest" syndrome. Your house will now be lacking sounds of loud music and teenage chatter on the telephone, and all the unexpected demands. Although you wished for years for peace and quiet while they were growing up, now you might find yourself saying, "I never heard so much quiet!" We may all yearn for "empty nest" experience, but when it does happen, we wonder why we wanted it in the first place.

This emptiness and silence in the home, compounded with missing the children, may at first induce unpleasant feelings. You may feel slightly depressed or suddenly feel older. Those feelings are a normal part of letting go of children and should dissipate in time. Keeping track of your children's progress away from home and helping them settle into their new life can compensate for their absence at home.

You may also feel a certain isolation from your spouse. Where the children occupied a good portion of your time before, now it is only you and your spouse and you don't know what to say to each other to fill the time. This too is a normal event in the life of a couple. It does not mean that you have nothing to talk about to each other. You can both learn to use this extra time to begin new conversations by tapping into each one's interests, hobbies, aspirations in life or creative ventures. This additional time together is an opportunity to get to know one another anew. It is a bonus time for both of you to enjoy and for renewing your commitment to one another.

Your New Social Life

You are also at the threshold of a social life unknown to you before. This social life can be filled with new or close friends, and family who enjoy your company and your contribution to their knowledge.

When you reach a pinnacle after having emerged from a life of doubts about being loved, your outlook on life is carefree. With a contented attitude on life, friends and people will gravitate around you. There is nothing more pleasing and uplifting than being with someone who is upbeat, who smiles and laughs at their own foibles or just laughs because they feel good.

You are also now at a milestone, at the unveiling of another world. Not the world you knew before that held nothing but doubts and frustration for you. This new world has awakened you to others who can benefit from your positive outlook on life and the creativity unleashed within you.

The tendency to be happy is contagious and when we have this natural gift we want to share it with others. That is where your contributions to society can have an impact. For example, in the past you may have been reluctant to help others and participate in causes because you felt you had nothing to contribute. Now, however, others will feel drawn to your calming and positive presence.

We become unbounded with radiant energy once our minds are clear and lightened. Your newfound energy will shine from within and reflect on others so they can receive it. You now will have the enthusiasm to help others and feel the contentment of being wanted and needed. As you reach this milestone you will see clearly into your life and soul. You will feel one with your immediate world and at peace with your place in the universe.

Your Financial Resources

At this time, what will your financial situation be and how will you provide for your retirement? Remember that the most productive years in potential earnings are between the ages of thirty-five and fifty-five. These high-potential earning years can be slowed down, halted or wiped out if you did not provide for them emotionally. Emotional problems, and the denial that they exist, can directly affect your earning potential. Think of the limitations that result when your physical strength is impaired. So too, your psychological health and how you tackle problems can make the difference between vegetating for lack of money and reaching your desired financial goals.

What are your resources right now? Are you still living in scarcity, tied up in debts and expenditures? You need to sit down and make a list of your assets and debts. Remember that debts accumulate interest and grow exponentially. Credit cards are the number one source of debts in this country. While buying on credit to acquire more possessions fuels the economy, it could also bring your house down. These and other debts can lead to anxiety and stress, undermining your blissful life.

Both you and your spouse need to take stock of your present financial situation and resources. One way to control debts is to put a lid on all spending for a few weeks or months. That will give you time to catch up on bills and pay down your debts. This belt-tightening can be endured by reminding both yourself and your spouse that you are enhancing your future economic wealth. Anything that you can save today will add to that wealth tomorrow.

Next you need to analyze all your assets to find ways of increasing them. There are excellent books on the subject of money management. Consulting a financial advisor is also worth the investment.

The Pinnacle: Self-Actualization

Now that you have taken care of your emotional well-being, have rediscovered love and are on your way to physical and financial health, you are ready for what psychologist Abraham Maslow called the highest need: the need for self-actualization. This is an individual need, creative in its own way that you can discover within yourself. Every individual reaches for their own self-actualization unlike any other individual. It is your own to discover. It is unique and no one can tell you what it is like or how to achieve it. By now all the steps you have taken in life have led you directly to this pinnacle of life's crowning. What you achieve is up to you.

A number of people in history reached heights of remarkable self-actualization. Some of those were leaders such as Moses, Christ, Mohammed, Gandhi, Mother Teresa, and other prophets. Their self-actualization brought them unconditional love with worldwide-reaching effects. While we may or may not achieve such heights of self-actualization, we can achieve our own standards of a self-actualized individual: love from our spouse, bliss, peace and serenity in our lives. This state of bliss is achieved by our own dedication to the noble cause of marriage: striving to make one individual happy and in turn creating our own happiness.

Exercise 24: My Self-Actualization Needs

Turn now to your journal and create a list of your own self-actualization needs. Summarize this list on an index card and title it "My Self-Actualization Needs."

Example

Highest   1.   Be the best that I can be.

               2.   Help others to find a path to happiness.

               3.   See to my children's happiness.

               4.   Find the love and bliss in my marriage.

Lowest   5.   Achieve emotional, physical and financial security.

Exercise Progress

Exercise 24 represents the highest level that you can achieve. You are now a self-individuated adult in full power and control of your life. By now you have accomplished your goal: to love your spouse and to be loved in return. You have now arrived at the crossroads where, on one path, life's misery and invalidation prevail, while on the other, spirituality and lightness of being dwell. You have chosen the right path, the one illuminated with love and with life.

Conclusion

Through the understanding of your past you have liberated yourself from earthly chains. You have now reached a stage in your life akin to the butterfly. The butterfly achieves a *spiritual metamorphosis* from chrysalis or cocoon to liberating freedom. It is this *spiritual ascendancy*, the transformation from earthly bounds to the freedom and uplifting of unimaginable heights, that brings *peace, wisdom* and *love.*

17

Living a Blissful Marriage

*The oath of inseparableness of two together, of
the woman that loves me and whom I love more
than my life, that oath swearing...*

—Walt Whitman

Visualize a center in your universe. This center is stable and radiates that stability from all directions. This center is also where harmony, bliss and peace live. Whenever you are in conflict with yourself or with your spouse, return to this center where the two of you are immersed in that bliss. That is the image you focus on when conflict occurs. Either one of you may distance from that center from time to time, but the magnetic pull back to this center will draw you there again.

This briefly is our goal in life: gravitation to a center of peace, harmony and bliss. See that center as your soul's retreat whenever you are in turmoil or life has dealt you a blow or you have lost sight of your reasons for being married. You can then ask yourself, what is real in my life and what is not? You need to look in the mirror of your spouse's humanity to rediscover the common bonds you have with him or her. This center then will hold all the keys and answers to your questions about married life, the paths you took in life and the changes you made accordingly.

Creating a Center of Peace

You can also physically create this harmonious center. You can set aside a corner in your home, or an entire room if you are fortunate to have the space, where you will retreat in times of conflict or confusion. This corner or room can be bathed in soft sunlight or lamplight. Around this space or room you can arrange images such as nature scenes, green forests, expansive ocean vistas, and murals depicting peace and harmony. Chimes or soft music can also enhance your mood.

This peaceful center then can become a retreat from life's harshness and turmoil. You and your spouse can approach puzzling questions or dead ends in your daily lives by returning to this center to renew yourselves.

The Volumes of Your Life

Picture this center, if you will, also as a library for your lives. That library will hold on its shelves the voluminous books describing every moment of your past lives. Other shelves will still be empty, waiting for you and your spouse to continue writing that life together. As you visualize these future volumes in your married life, you can let your minds wander and be emboldened with all the possibilities and marvelous aspects of life awaiting the two of you.

From time to time, the written volumes of your married life need to be dusted and reviewed. You can review the beginnings of your married life by remembering all the moments you and your spouse spent together—the joys, frustrations, letdowns, momentous occasions, arguments, reconciliations, and forgiveness. These events that knocked you down, and then uplifted you, contributed to making you the individuals you are today. They molded your character, as iron is molded by the blacksmith's hammer.

These experiences gave you the determination to reconstruct your lives together and forge a stronger and permanent foundation.

Human beings are fallible. They make mistakes but can also forgive and ask for forgiveness, and continually change their lives for the betterment of all. The moment you rediscovered your soul-mate by merging through their fallibility and vulnerability, you then become one in your life goals. While each one of you is a separate entity, you are both the same in your search for love and bliss.

At the Pinnacle of Bliss

Order and serenity for you and your spouse can be achieved by eliminating conflicts and stress and all your life's energies can then be channeled to reach higher pinnacles.

As order comes into your life, you will congratulate yourself for having taken the road less traveled. This is the road to self-discovery by facing the truths about yourself, as painful as they may be. Once you realize that a painful past can prevent you from living in the moment, this knowledge can never hurt you again. The unleashing of past emotional hurts can no longer use up your precious vital energies. This newfound energy can now be re-channeled into loving your husband or wife and spending your remaining years together in blissful moments.

The number one tool you have used to reach these heights is merging with your spouse, and understanding that both of you are vulnerable and that you share this vulnerability in common with others. Other tools that you have used, and will continue to use, are introspection, examination of irrational thoughts and behaviors, and modification of those behaviors through journal writing and reviewing your index cards. In spite of all odds and the recurring stages of conflict in marriage, the true test in staying married is not to walk away but to sit down and resolve issues by keeping the door open to communication to reach a solution.

The important thing to remember is that conflicts will arise from time to time even though you are in love and your marriage has reached the blissful stage. We are human; we have our ups and downs and sometimes we falter. However, we now possess the tools and the understanding that marriage is sacred and needs to be nurtured to survive.

Marriage constantly redefines itself through the years, and both husband and wife can surmount its hurdles by being compliant to its goal yet fluid enough to move within its limits. If you find yourself wanting more help with puzzling issues and seek out additional books on relationships, or therapy or counseling, that will be a positive progression in your life. With changing times, life unfolds and brings new challenges and new questions into our lives. An effective way of adapting to a changing life is to continually seek answers to troubling questions.

When bliss is present in the marriage, it unlocks the door to discovery into each other's soul. Among the treasures you and your spouse may experience are synchronous moments when your thoughts are the same, times when your laughter will lift you and give you that special lightness of being, and moments of ecstasy when your two bodies feel as one in sexual love.

Bliss in the marriage means not only making constant and exciting new discoveries every day in your partner, but also discovering the deeper meaning of safety. Part of the commitment that two people make to each other, and to the relationship, is to let the other breathe in a free space within the marriage. Above all, the marriage was created out of the need of two people to be together, merge in partnership, bring children into the world and continue to renew their lives through them into immortality.

I would like to digress for a moment to recount a personal experience. After my aunt Lilian Prince passed away in 1998, I discovered a special tape among her possessions. On that tape was the voice of my uncle Fred, her husband of many years, who had died only a short time before her. It was a magical moment for me to hear his voice again:

> "During all our years we found a deep satisfaction and a great concern for each other. Now after five and a half decades, we are the survivors of a marriage that will continue. There must be a formula that held this relationship together. We believe, in our own case, that it was the one thousand acts of kindness. That was the reservoir and the training ground that sustained us. We think the past was good and now we will add tonight and tomorrow, two more perfect days with our families to celebrate our fifty-fifth wedding anniversary."

Fifty-five years of marriage is indeed an achievement. However, any number of years in a couple's married life can also be an accomplishment if they are lived with the purpose of devoting themselves to each other. You and your spouse can also reach those heights through the knowledge of your histories and learning the art of patience with life's struggles.

By the same token, we must also remember that we are all as precious as priceless diamonds. Through the years, we become polished and grow in value. We also grow in awareness, becoming increasingly attuned to the world around us, and reach the higher plane of a spiritual life. When all these ideals have been met, bliss within the marriage will lead us to find the spirituality of soul in lives well lived.

References

Bender, Sue. *Everyday Sacred*. (pp. 85). New York: Harper Collins, 1995.

Burgess, Alan. From THE SMALL WOMAN by Alan Burgess, copyright © 1957 by E.P. Dutton, renewed © 1985 by Alan Burgess. Used by permission of Dutton, a division of Penguin Putnam Inc. 21-23.
The Inn of the Sixth Happiness. The Movie. Twentieth Century Fox Film Corp, 1958.

Capel, Anne K., Markoe, Glenn E., Editors. Essays by Catharine H. Roehrig, Betsy M. Bryan, and Janet H. Johnson. Reprinted from *Mistress of the House, Mistress of Heaven: Women in ancient Egypt* by permission of the publisher, New York: Hudson Hills Press. © 1996 by Cincinnati Art Museum. Betsy M. Bryan. Lectures Series. Los Angeles, 1999.

Carlson, Neil R. *Foundations of Physiological Psychology* (pp. 2, 25, 88-95, 313-318 Table 4.1). Needham Heights, Massachusetts: Simon & Schuster Company, 1995.

Carroll, J., Volk, K., & Hyde, J. (1985). Differences between males and females in motives for engaging in sexual intercourse. *Archives of Sexual Behavior*, 14, 131-139.

Clark, R., & Hatfield, E. (1989). Gender differences in receptivity to sexual offers. *Journal of Psychology and Human Differences*, 2, 39-55.

Crooks, R., & Baur, K. (1993). *Our Sexuality*. Fifth Edition. Pacific Grove, California: Brooks/Cole Publishing Company, (pp. 187-188, 196, 482-484).

Freud, Anna. *The Ego and Mechanisms of Defense*. Madison, Connecticut: International University Press, 1966.

Freud, Sigmund. *Inhibitions, Symptoms and Anxiety*. (pp. xxx-xxxi, xxix-xxxi). New York: W.W. Norton & Company, 1959, 1989.

_____,*The Ego and the Id* (pp.xxii-xxiii). New York. W.W. Norton & Company. 1960. Sigmund Freud: A Brief Life. Biographical Introduction by Peter Gay, 1989.

Gibran, Khalil. *The Prophet* (pp.17). New York: Alfred A. Knopf, 1976.

Hughes, Langston. 1987. "Dream Deferred" and "Still Here". From COLLECTED POEMS by Langston Hughes. Copyright © 1994 by the Estate of Langston Hughes. Reprinted by permission of Alfred A. Knopf, a Division of Random House, Inc. 14, 23.

Leigh, B. (1989). Reasons for having and avoiding sex: Gender, sexual orientation, and relationship to sexual behavior. *Journal of Sex Research*, 26, 199-208.

Levin, Ira. *The Stepford Wives*. New York. Random House. 1972.

Levine, S. "Intrapsychic and interpersonal aspects of impotence: Psychogenic erectile dysfunction." 1992. In R. Rosen & S. Leiblum (Eds.), *Erectile Disorders*. New York: Guilford Press.

_____, & Althof, S. "The pathogenesis of psychogenic erectile dysfunction." *Journal of Sex Education & Therapy*, 4, 251-266.

Merriam-Webster's Collegiate® Dictionary, Tenth Edition © 2000 by Merriam-Webster, Incorporated., 714. Springfield, Massachusetts. 1987.

Monte, Christopher F. *Beneath the Mask* [pp. 7, 78-88, (197-199 rights owned by International Universities Press) 303-307, 131-137, 684-685, 704]. Orlando, Florida: Harcourt Brace Jovanovich, Inc.

Quadagno, D. & Sprague, J. (1991). Reasons for having sex. *Medical Aspects of Human Sexuality*, June, 52.

Roddenberry, Gene. *Star Trek*. Paramount Pictures; 1969. "Let That Be Your Last Battle " (pp.123). *In The Star Trek Compendium*. New York: Pocket Books. (1989).

Rogers, Carl. (1957). Beneath the Mask. Christopher Monte. (1991). Harcourt Brace Jovanovich. (pp. 704).

Steele, Edward J., Lindley, Robyn A., Blanden, Robert V. *Lamarck's Signature: How Retrogenes Are Changing Darwin's Natural Selection Paradigm* (pp.5-6). Perseus Books. 1998.

Newspaper Articles

Los Angeles Times. (1996). "National Center for Health Statistics." (1988).

Los Angeles Times. (1998). "Effects of Parents' Split on children Is Divided" (A16).

Warren, Jennifer. (1998). "No-Fault Divorce Under Fire in State Nation." (A1-16). *Los Angeles Times*.

GENEALOGY CHART
(Sample for photocopying)

YOU:

NAME_____

PROFESSION_____

MARITAL STATUS_____

BEHAVIOR_____

DREAMS_____

REGRETS_____

FATHER: **MOTHER:**

Name   _____   _____

Profession   _____   _____

M. Status   _____   _____

Behavior   _____   _____

Dreams   _____   _____

Regrets   _____   _____

UNCLE:

Name _____   **UNCLE:** _____

Name _____

Profession _____   _____

M. Status _____   _____

Behavior _____   _____

Dreams _____   _____

Regrets _____   _____

AUNT:

Name _____   **AUNT:** _____

Profession _____   _____

M. Status _____   _____

Behavior _____   _____

Dreams _____   _____

Regrets _____   _____

GRANDPARENTS: **GRANDPARENTS:**

	Grand-father	Grand-mother	Grand-father	Grand-mother
Name	_____		_____	
Prof.	_____		_____	
M.S.	_____		_____	
Behav.	_____		_____	
Dreams	_____		_____	
Regrets	_____		_____	

Similar Traits or Behavior

You: Relative:

_____   _____

_____   _____

_____   _____

_____   _____

_____   _____

_____   _____

_____   _____

_____   _____

_____   _____

_____   _____

_____   _____

_____   _____

_____   _____

_____   _____

_____   _____

_____   _____

_____   _____

_____   _____

_____   _____

CHILDREN:

Child #1.

Name_____

Your expectations and dreams for them_____

_____

Their expectations and dreams_____

_____

My contributions to help them achieve their dreams_____

_____

Child #2.

Name_____

Your expectations and dreams for them_____

_____

Their expectations and dreams_____

_____

My contributions to help them achieve their dreams_____

_____

Child #3.

Name_____

Your expectations and dreams for them_____

_____

Their expectations and dreams_____

_____

My contributions to help them achieve their dreams_____

_____

Index

Motivational Cards

14 Inspirational Reminder-cards
to help keep your marriage on track.
(each 3x5 inches, laminated, in plastic case)

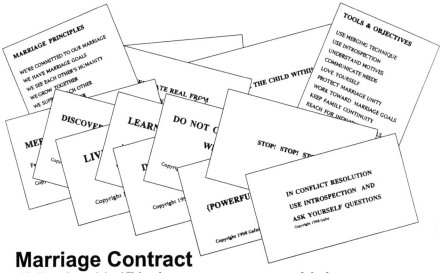

Marriage Contract
(full-color, 11x17 inches,
suitable for framing)

Living a
Blissful Marriage
Bookmark
(3x8 Inches, laminated)

(Order Form on next page)

Order Form

☎ **Telephone orders: (310) 544-6223**
(Have your credit card ready)

🖷 **Fax Orders: (310) 377-5203**

🖳 **E-mail orders: LILfinbk@netscape.net**

🖻 **Mail orders: Lifeline Publishing**
PO Box 4689
Palos Verdes Peninsula, CA 90274

	Quantity	Amount
Living a Blissful Marriage (BOOK) **$16.95**	_____	_____
Marriage Contract (Full-color) **$12.95** (11x17 inches, suitable for framing)	_____	_____
Motivational Cards (Laminated) **$9.95**	_____	_____
Bookmark (Laminated) **$5.95**	_____	_____
U.S. Priority Shipping & Handling $4.00 first item ($2.00 each additional)		_____
International Shipping & Handling $9.00 first item ($5.00 each additional)		_____
California addresses add 8.25% sales tax		_____
Total Amount enclosed (U.S. Funds)		_____

Company Name:_____

Name:_____

Address:_____

City:_____ **State:**_____ **Zip:**_____

Telephone:_____ **E-mail:**_____

Payment:

❏ **Check**   ❏ **MasterCard**   ❏ **Visa**

❏ **Optima**   ❏ **AMEX**   ❏ **Discover**

Card number:_____ **Exp. date:**____/____

Name on card:_____